Project Management for Information Professionals

CHANDOS
INFORMATION PROFESSIONAL SERIES

Series Editor: Ruth Rikowski
(email: Rikowskigr@aol.com)

Chandos' new series of books is aimed at the busy information professional. They have been specially commissioned to provide the reader with an authoritative view of current thinking. They are designed to provide easy-to-read and (most importantly) practical coverage of topics that are of interest to librarians and other information professionals. If you would like a full listing of current and forthcoming titles, please visit www.chandospublishing.com.

New authors: we are always pleased to receive ideas for new titles; if you would like to write a book for Chandos, please contact Dr Glyn Jones on g.jones.2@ elsevier.com or telephone +44 (0) 1865 843000.

Project Management for Information Professionals

MARGOT NOTE

Amsterdam • Boston • Cambridge • Heidelberg
London • New York • Oxford • Paris • San Diego
San Francisco • Singapore • Sydney • Tokyo
Chandos Publishing is an imprint of Elsevier

Chandos Publishing is an imprint of Elsevier
225 Wyman Street, Waltham, MA 02451, USA
Langford Lane, Kidlington, OX5 1GB, UK

ISBN: 978-0-08-100127-1 (print)
ISBN: 978-0-08-100133-2 (online)

British Library Cataloguing-in-Publication Data
A catalogue record for this book is available from the British Library

Library of Congress Control Number: 2015946210

For information on all Chandos Publishing publications
visit our website at http://store.elsevier.com/

Working together
to grow libraries in
developing countries

www.elsevier.com • www.bookaid.org

CONTENTS

ABOUT THE AUTHOR

Margot Note has spent her career working in the cultural heritage sector, including colleges, libraries, and archives. She has lead or has participated in a wide range of projects, including database conversions, digitization efforts, web application creations, and collaborations with American Express, Artstor, Google, and UNESCO. She holds a Masters in History from Sarah Lawrence College, a Masters in Library and Information Science, and a Post-Master's Certificate in Archives and Records Management, both from Drexel University. She is the Director of Archives and Information Management at World Monuments Fund, an international heritage conservation organization.

The author can be contacted via the publisher.

ACKNOWLEDGMENTS

Books, like projects, are rarely completed in solitude. Many people have contributed to the creation of this publication. Thanks to the Florio, Leis, and Note families. I would like to thank the staff of the Pelham Bay branch of the New York Public Library for keeping their hold shelf full of project management books for me, week after week. I have much appreciation for Larry Blake, who generously shared his project management experience with me throughout the course of writing this book. Thank you most of all to my partner, Bill Florio, for being supportive of me during the writing process.

This book is dedicated to the memory of my father, Charles C. Note (1945–2015).

INTRODUCTION

Thrown into deep end b/c of compe- tence

Project Management for Information Professionals is a resource for people who have not been trained formally in project management principles, yet have found themselves involved in projects. They could be working on a recataloging endeavor at their library, directing their colleagues in a digitization effort in their archives, or establishing a new content management system at their museum. Colleagues may have sought them out because of their leadership abilities. They may have earned their assignments because they are dependable, good at organizing their work, and skilled at influencing others. Given increasing amounts of responsibility over time, they get things done in changing information environments.

Projects require collaboration between departments and across enterprises. Sometimes they involve traversing boundaries—professional, organizational, geographical, or technological. This dynamic creates a need for information professionals to work in partnership, communicate effectively, and appreciate the best practices of project management. Information professionals often accomplish projects alongside their regular duties, and find they need to develop innovative skills to balance their workloads. The opportunity to take responsibility for a project offers personal and career development and the prospect of achieving lasting change and impact.

Often a library, archives or museum must undertake a project that is outside its normal operations, but is essential for it to fulfill its strategic goals. All change in organizations happens through projects. Entrenching a project management mindset in the organization's culture is the way to make this happen.

Project-based work in archives, libraries, and museums is on the rise for several reasons. Project management has the potential to be the métier of information professionals. The principles, structures, and processes of project management are analogous to library and information science; both are logical, methodical, measurable, and specific (Massis, 2010).

There has been an increase in technology-based work, such as the implementation of integrated library systems, digital repositories, and open-source applications. As information centers become partners in larger, more complex projects within their communities, there is likely to be a greater reliance on project management methodologies to reach favorable outcomes (Wamsley, 2009). Kinkus (2007) adds:

> Not only does the progression of technology seem to be introducing more opportunities for project-based work in libraries, but the increased complexity caused by a project's need for expertise from multiple departments leads to an increased need for project management skills in modern librarian jobs (p. 357).

Archives and museums have surmounted contemporary challenges with project management techniques as well.

Projects are integral to efforts to respond to a rapidly changing environment. In the current climate of diminished funding, information professionals need to maximize available resources and minimize risks in their projects. They encounter challenges in resource formats, diverse patrons, and evolving technology platforms and interfaces. Much of the work of professionals employed in archives, libraries, and museums involves projects that cross departments. Additionally, today's workforce values the skill of being able to manage project team members without formal authority. Increasing demand for technology implementation in library, archives, and museum operations and expanded user services has occurred at the same time that most budgets and staff sizes have decreased. In a business environment that requires doing more with less, information professionals who master project management demonstrate their worth by getting things done under these exigent conditions. This is where project management comes into play.

LITERATURE REVIEW

Project management is an essential part of the work of information professionals, although it is only just starting to be recognized. Chambers and Perrow (1998) surveyed librarians in the United Kingdom and discovered that 27% used specific project management techniques, including schedules, Gantt charts, and network diagrams. They found that 3% of the respondents used formal project management methodologies. This may suggest that information professionals are beginning to see the value of using practical project management techniques.

In their survey of web project management in academic libraries, Fagan and Keach (2011) found the repeated use of project management practices, but without proper job titles, recognition, or methodologies. They write:

> The function of project management is still often only one part of a hybrid job and is not often included in job descriptions. Some project management techniques are used frequently, but the most formal practices are not (p. 1).

However, the results of their survey showed significant use of specific procedures:

> More than 90% of respondents "frequently" or "sometimes" document project requirements and specifications, and more than 80% archive documents for future project teams, identify milestones, and submit project status reports. These findings are encouraging, as these activities support good organizational communication about projects (p. 19).

Not surprisingly, they found that practices focusing on description and documentation align with information professionals' traditional strengths in preserving knowledge.

As Schachter (2004) explains, information professionals "don't often call ourselves project managers, but the fact that we do so much project management... is increasingly being acknowledged and promoted as a core skill set of librarianship" (p. 10). Lai (2005) investigated the needed educational background and expertise for knowledge management professionals, many of whom hold library and information science (LIS) degrees. In reviewing job postings, she found project management expertise was one of the top three skills required; she noted its occurrence in 48.2% of 27 full-time listings from 2000 to 2001. Kinkus (2007) analyzed library job advertisements and found an increase from 4.1% to 11.2% in jobs requiring project management skills from 1993 to 2003. She writes, "Based on surveys of both librarian job ads and MLIS curricula, it is clear that project management in libraries is here to stay" (p. 352). Mathews and Pardue (2009) investigated librarian advertisements and noted that 29.5% specified project management skills. In a similar survey of more than 300 job advertisements from 1999 to 2007, Choi and Rasmussen (2009) found 37.93% of LIS positions focused on projects.

While information professionals frequently lead, coordinate, and participate in many projects, most LIS programs overlook project management training. Winston and Hoffman (2005) published an analysis of library school curricula for evidence of project management instruction. Contrary to the need for project management skills in the profession, they discovered that only 3.7% of the 56 programs investigated offered project management courses. Similarly, Mackenzie and Smith (2009) found that of the 24 course syllabi from 17 ALA-accredited graduate library programs, only 12.5% included project management as one of the topics taught in their management courses.

Little formal project mgmt training; prof dev, or on the job

In a study focused on jobs, curricula, and programs in analyzing the education of future "'eScience Professionals' who extend librarianship into solving large scale information management problems for researchers and engineers," Stanton et al. (2011) write:

> The extent to which project management skills seemed to figure prominently in all of the students, internships suggested that project management ought to be a required course for anyone seeking to become an eScience professional (pp. 79, 89).

At the other end of the professional spectrum, art librarianship also requires project management mastery:

> In all environments project management is a popular tool for accomplishing specific goals. In the visual resources field these tasks may include digitizing, organizing, and providing access for specific collections. The popularity of digitization projects and the increased number of funding sources have resulted in a large number of these activities being undertaken in all visual resources environments. In addition, institutions have also recognized the value of digital access to collections and as such are increasingly supporting such endeavors. As a result, project management has become a necessary skill (Iyer, 2009).

These studies suggest that project management is often required for information professionals in the workplace, although it is not being taught enough in graduate programs.

Although formal education has not caught up with project management needs, LIS resources devoted to project management have increased. For example, articles, workshops, and books such as this one have added to the collective wisdom of the field. This supports the belief that collaboration and managerial ability, two keystones of project management, are significant to the development of information professionals (Brasley, 2008). Black (2005) comments, "There is little training within the museum field for managing major projects through to completion—mostly people have to learn on the job" (p. 224). Information professionals are using professional development opportunities to advance skills absent in graduate school. In the future, all LIS curricula will provide project management courses, allowing students to participate in and lead projects before they enter the working world.

The professional literature describes several cases of libraries using project management methodologies. For example, in 2008 the libraries at the University of Arizona formally adopted a project planning and managing process overseen by a portfolio management group, which is a subcommittee of the library leadership cabinet. This group ensures projects meet the libraries' strategic goals and priorities (Feeney and Sult, 2011). The group "is responsible for ensuring that programs and projects are strategic in nature, aligned with Libraries' goals, and that resources are allocated to the highest-priority programs and projects" (Stoffle and Cuillier, 2011, p. 155). Universities in the United States, Ireland, England, and Australia have also reported cases of effective use of project management methodologies (Horwath, 2012).

Most information professionals balance technology with serving people, which makes them ideal candidates to be project managers. Additionally, they are suited for project management due to their expertise in planning, supervision, and analysis. Wamsley (2009) notes that information professionals implement services, upgrade systems, and build community partnerships, and that "all of these activities involve project work and the need for library staff to have [project management] knowledge and skills" (p. 5).

For the information professional, the key to success in a changing environment is to develop the new skills that the workplace demands. Above all, information professionals must actively prioritize a commitment to continuous professional development. The information industry is growing fast, and the profession is experiencing rapid change. Project management can assist in developing much-needed skills to compete and thrive in this setting. *A structure for practice amidst flux, a framework for exercising judgment about how best to manage a project*

WHY I WROTE THIS BOOK

In my experience with working on projects in nonprofits, libraries, and archives, I noticed a pattern. When I directed a project in which I was the primary worker, I was organized, within budget, and on time. I sensed when I could solve problems on my own and when I should consult senior executives. I envisioned the workflow and processes it would take to deliver results. These projects were always successful.

However, as my career advanced I got involved in bigger projects: either leading them myself or working as a member of a team. Now, things were different. I had to handle diverse personalities, competing priorities and schedules, various seniority levels, and organizational politics. The project results were often satisfactory, but occasionally they were not. The process was sometimes unpleasant. I wondered if there was a better way.

Out of curiosity and a need for self-improvement, I began to study project management literature. I found that most current research focused on project management in the corporate sector and did not address the unique problems of managing projects in libraries, archives, and museums. I wanted to apply what I had learned to provide a resource that would speak to information professionals. I started a journey that culminated in this volume.

This book offers a summary of project management principles without the need to read traditional project management literature. These publications are written for corporate audiences in companies with assigned project managers or project management offices. I have created a book focusing on the techniques that will influence work in archives, libraries, and museums. The focus on nonprofit organizations is essential because funding, staff, and time are limited.

Additionally, the environments that information professionals tend to work in concentrate more on improving services and reducing costs, rather than the revenue-generating goals of the corporate world. Information professionals create websites for online catalogs, digitize holdings, or initiate library programs, rather than build multimillion-dollar pieces of military equipment or produce goods for the global market. However, the methods used for all circumstances are the same.

My goal in writing this book is to provide a resource for those who are leading or contributing to projects, but may not have the knowledge and skills to participate in their fullest capacity yet. I hope that after reading this volume and consulting the resources I provide, readers will feel this book fills the lacuna of knowledge in the profession.

PURPOSE OF THIS BOOK

This book will enable readers to learn the theories and techniques of project management, which will help them to understand user needs, work with vendors, and communicate with stakeholders throughout the project life cycle. Readers will discover how to select, plan, and execute projects in the real world.

The demands placed on organizations today affect an individual's approach to work. In dynamic, service-oriented, technology-rich work environments such as libraries, archives, and museums, information professionals must be competent in their fields of expertise and in their ability to solve problems, pursue opportunities, and affect change. Speed, change, lower costs, complexity, and uncertainty characterize the contemporary work environment. This presents daunting challenges, but project management grants the flexibility to adapt technical and soft skills to the situation at hand.

Since every institution and project is different, the book does not prescribe specific technologies or procedures. Additionally, an unavoidable risk when writing about technology is that references to products, computer hardware specifications, current standards, and other details can become outdated quickly. There is no right way to lead projects; there are only best practices that inform decisions based on the nature of the projects, institutional missions, available resources, technical infrastructures, and user requirements. Knowledge about a variety of approaches allows project managers to make the appropriate choices that are right for their institutions.

SCOPE

This book provides a balance between theory and practice to assist readers in opting for strategies that best meet the current and projected needs of their institutions. While the book aims to be as comprehensive as possible, the coverage has had to be selective. Certain topics are covered in a cursory fashion, although they could easily be the subjects of entire books. The contents of *Project Management for Information Professionals* should be viewed as the chief areas within a larger territory of inquiry.

AUDIENCE

Throughout the book, I use the phrase "information professionals," rather than "archivists," "librarians," or "curators." Information professionals are people who use information strategically to advance the mission of their organizations through the development, distribution, and management of information resources and services. The use of this term is meant to be inclusive of all those who work in some information capacity, regardless of education or professional background.

Traditionally, archives, libraries, and museums have had different ways of organizing, documenting, and preserving their collections. However, with the emergence of digitization as the primary tool for preservation and presentation of cultural artifacts, distinctions between the institutions blur (Kirchhoff et al., 2008). In addition, many believe that the commonalities of these institutions are more significant than their differences (Whiteman, 2007; Bak and Armstrong, 2009). This book focuses on how information professionals in memory institutions can improve their project management knowledge and skills despite the type of institution they work at or the collections they manage.

Many who read this book may not have set career goals to become project managers, but they may need to know how to manage projects to advance in their careers. Even though they realize they need tools, techniques, and knowledge to handle new assignments, they may be unable to devote much time to acquiring project management skills. This book was created to assist professionals in the field with limited time and resources.

The book requires no previous knowledge of project work and should appeal to anyone in the library, archives, or museum communities interested in developing project management skills, including students and new graduates. It is for employees who have never been on a project team and those who have just entered the workforce, as well as experienced project managers and people who have had years of real-world experience.

CERTIFICATION

I wrote this book for those who want to learn enough about project management methodologies to ensure that their projects succeed. Those interested in certification in the field should consult the most widely known reference of project management best practices: *A Guide to the Project Management Body of Knowledge* (PMBOK), published by the Project Management Institute (PMI). Founded in 1965, the PMI develops standards and offers certifications in project management. The fifth and most recent edition of PMBOK (PMBOK 5) was published in 2013. The Project Management Professional (PMP) certification includes an examination administered by PMI with questions based on PMBOK 5. While *Project Management for Information Professionals* will provide guidelines on project management, it will not assist readers in certification. The PMBOK is the authority in the field and an essential resource for project management mastery.

ORGANIZATION OF THIS BOOK

This book is divided into sections that correspond to the keys to successful project management: initiating, planning, executing, controlling, and closing. The chapters are roughly arranged in order. Projects, however, do not progress from one logical stage to another. Those who are managing a project for the first time may find it useful to glance through the chapters and note the issues that are raised so that the book supports learning needs.

Chapter 1 provides an overview of project management. I define what a project is, as well as characterizing aspects of project management. The benefits of project management are also examined.

Chapter 2 explores how to select a suitable project and determine its goals and objectives. At this stage, formulating strategies, gathering requirements, and clarifying success criteria are crucial. Readers will also learn to formulate a scope statement and consider assumptions and risks that may affect the success of the project.

Chapter 3 focuses on people, one of the most rewarding aspects of project management. In this chapter readers will learn what it takes to become a project manager, develop leadership skills, and work with stakeholders. It discusses developing the team and determining team member roles. Evaluating performance, tracking progress, and managing expectations are also decisive skills to be examined.

Planning and scheduling the project are the focus of Chapter 4. Preparing the plan, developing the work breakdown structure, and defining the sequence of work are critical project management skills. Establishing the schedule, executing the plan, and procuring resources are the next steps for success.

Chapter 5 provides an overview of budgeting and performance. Readers will determine the budget and calculate costs with estimation methods. They will examine the cost of quality and evaluate performance. Additionally, they will maintain control, review costs, and manage change.

Communication and documentation throughout the project life cycle fill Chapter 6. Readers will understand how to write a project charter, establish a communication plan, and report on project performance. Communicating with the team, handling problems, and generating status reports are also examined.

Chapter 7 covers completion of the project and review. Readers are advised on how to verify the scope, manage claims, and close the project. Producing final reports, recognizing lessons learned, and rewarding the team are also discussed. Sections on managing transitions and creating project archives finish the chapter.

Five appendices supply additional pertinent information. Appendix A presents a series of questions, an *aide mémoire* to be considered before commencing a project. Further sources of project management information in books and websites are offered in Appendix B. URLs are current as of

vivid, precise language

September 2015. Appendix C provides a list of software programs for managing projects. Appendix D contains a glossary of project management terms. Finally, Appendix E provides templates of standard project management forms. A template library reduces planning time, increases the quality of the project management experience, and decreases the risk of project failure. Additional benefits include increasing standard practices, developing learning modules for new project managers, and establishing an archives of project artifacts. The book also contains figures to elaborate upon issues raised in the text and serve as a reference for future use.

GETTING STARTED

This book demonstrates how to apply project management to the development of information projects. It recognizes that the individual members of a project team are likely to be different. They have diverse skills and levels of competence and require varying degrees of supervision, so the work activities need to suit the individual.

The book also recognizes that team members work best in an organized and stable environment where ground rules are established in advance and do not change to suit the whim of others. If project managers wish to deliver a high-quality project on time and within budget, there are many ways of doing it right. *habits of thought & practice*

Knowledge alone does not make a project manager. The application of project management methodology produces a winning project. Project management skills and techniques are not burdensome tasks to be performed because some processes require it. Rather, they are a way of thinking, communicating, and executing. They are an integral part of how information professionals approach aspects of their work every day to resolve the Gordian knots of their projects.

If you have leadership skills in addition to a systematic approach, your success will be possible, but leadership alone is insufficient. This book will help you to add the essential professionalism which is the foundation for success.

Project managers in and outside the information profession have found that project management is a learn-by-doing endeavor in which improvements come only from experience. If you put into place the strategies that this book describes, then your projects are more likely to end successfully. You will be able to make commitments on budgets and schedules with confidence, and deliver on your promises. You will build a record of accomplishment with consistent project triumph.

I hope everyone reading this book will wonder why all projects are not well managed, because these techniques are straightforward and easy to use. I also assume readers recognize that a difference exists between knowing what to do and actually doing it. Project management is an art and a science. The art is strongly tied to interpersonal aspects, while the science comprises an understanding of processes, tools, and techniques. I have assembled in this book a set of principles that work well in practice and have been applied to projects large and small. If you follow the guidelines thoroughly, you will be a long way toward achieving success. I believe that the knowledge imparted in this book will allow you to lead and participate in many triumphant projects in the libraries, archives, and museums that employ you.

CHAPTER 1

Project Management Overview

Delightful and apt epigrams!

Begin at the beginning, and go on till you come to the end: then stop.

Lewis Carroll, Alice in Wonderland

We are continually faced with a series of great opportunities brilliantly disguised as insoluble problems.

John W. Gardner, former US Secretary of Health, Education, and Welfare

It must be considered that there is nothing more difficult to carry out, nor more doubtful of success, nor more dangerous to handle, than to initiate a new order of things.

Niccolò Machiavelli, The Prince

1.1 WHAT IS A PROJECT?

A project is a series of unique, multifaceted, and related activities with a purpose that must be accomplished at a particular time, within cost constraints, and according to specifications. Although different projects have common features, each project has a specific one-off set of attributes (Table 1.1). A project happens once and creates something to be completed by a given deadline. It is initiated, builds or transforms something, and leaves behind the outcome of the work. To be judged as successful, a project must be on schedule, within budget, complete with agreed-upon functions, and of suitable quality. At the project's end, the outputs of the work are handed over to the day-to-day operations of the organization.

Theoretically, a project is unique because no two projects are alike. Even if the same method is being used to create something, the personalities of people and their agendas will change the shaping of the outcome. Project managers may not have access to a wealth of historical information when they start a project. They may have to launch their projects with limited information or misinformation. *Projects vs. programs*

In some organizations, projects may be managed together in a program to obtain benefits and control that are unavailable from managing them individually. Programs are sets of correlated projects that are achieved using project management techniques in a coordinated fashion. When organizations administer projects collectively as programs, they capitalize on

Project Management for Information Professionals
ISBN 978-0-08-100127-1

Table 1.1 Project Attributes

- Has a goal
- Has a timeframe
- Has a budget
- Has specifications
- Has a result
- Requires a plan
- Requires resources
- Is unique
- Is complex
- Forges connections between departments
- Can be evaluated

---

benefits that would not be achievable if the projects were managed separately. Programs have larger scopes or more significant benefits than single projects. Programs are usually phased, with the target end dates of the initial stages well defined. Subsequent phases are demarcated as the first phase approaches completion, enabling new related projects to be initiated.

Institutions may prioritize multiple programs into portfolios aligned with significant strategic objectives so that resources can be applied promptly. A portfolio groups projects and programs together to facilitate the achievement of specific strategic business objectives. Portfolio management administers active programs and projects along with future opportunities to ensure the resources of the organization are deployed to achieve strategic objectives. Portfolio managers consider the value of each potential project against the organization's strategic objectives. They also monitor active projects for adherence to objectives, balance the portfolio among the other investments of the organization, and manage the efficient use of resources.

Organizations execute a multitude of activities as part of the work aimed at achieving objectives. Some of these activities support projects, and others sustain operations; the attributes of both differ (Table 1.2). An operation is a set of functions that do not qualify as a project. An operation performs ongoing tasks; it does not produce something new, nor does it have a beginning or an end. Therefore, it is not a project. Projects differ from the continuing operations of an organization in that they are temporary and unique. These qualities mean that factors like personnel, lines of authority, budgeting, accounting, and communication need to be handled differently in the project environment. Organizations may fund projects and operations out of the same budgets and use many of the same people. Both

Table 1.2 Differences between Projects and Operations

Projects	Operations
Definite beginning and ending	No definite beginning and ending
Temporary endeavor	Ongoing endeavor
Unique output	Repetitive output
Project roles and responsibilities	Standing roles and responsibilities
Diverse skills	Specialist skills
Dynamic teams	Functional teams aligned with organizational structure
Cost constraints	Annual budget
Estimated time and costs	Fixed events and set budgets
Ending determined by specific criteria	Processes are repeated many times

require a broad range of the same management skills: written and oral communication, conflict resolution, motivation, accounting, and negotiating. However, these similarities can obscure the real differences between projects and operations. Recognizing these variances leads to a better understanding of their challenges. Projects have unique problems that require various management disciplines. The project management techniques discussed throughout this book have evolved to meet these challenges.

Projects could include moving a library, creating an intranet site, digitizing a collection, restructuring an information service, or carrying out research in an innovative area. Conversely, operations may include managing staff members, submitting payroll, running a reading room, or administrating an interlibrary loan program.

Whether an organization launches a project to pursue an opportunity, solve a problem, or fulfill an unmet need, it commits time, money, and human resources to achieve its goal. The goal spawns the objectives that the project must attain and helps determine its scope. When the goal is unambiguous and the objectives are well defined, it is easy to tell when the project is complete.

Projects are investments and produce beneficial results, which are described in a number of ways. One approach is to justify a project because it ensures organizational survival. This type of project is mandatory rather than discretionary. It must be done to comply with government or industry standards or to sustain operational readiness. Fixing a leaking roof or making a facility accessible to people with disabilities would fall into this category.

Other projects might contribute to improved value—they may provide better cost controls, system upgrades, streamlined workflows, or improved user satisfaction. Projects in this area could include office relocations, organizational restructuring, or launching a new capital campaign. Finally, some projects try to secure the long-term growth of the organization. These strategic projects may start new services in an archives or deploy new or emerging technologies in a museum.

Projects define what they are going to deliver in tangible means or in an intangible change that has to be made measurable. For example, constructing a new archives and special collections center with all the systems, facilities, and furniture that go into the building is a concrete change. However, improving programming services for teens at the library necessitates the invention of identifiable outcomes that indicate you have succeeded. For example, metrics about young adult material circulation, event attendance, and summer reading program registrations demonstrate the positive improvements from the project that advance the organization. For service industries like the information professions, it is important to measure management effectiveness because most projects involve improving services, not creating products.

Projects are challenging because organizations are doing something they have never done before. By their nature, projects have elements of discovery in them, as processes for achieving results are inimitable. Projects are out of the ordinary, so their problems, restrictions, deadlines, and budgets are outside the regular course of operations. Projects always produce change. Since every project is different from the last one, project managers cannot depend on what has worked before. The secret to execution is both the development of new skills and the application of existing expertise to a new environment.

Projects present novel demands that require commitments from limited resources. Information professionals are expected to continue meeting their recurring work activities as they pursue project goals. Thus projects place additional burdens on those performing the work. If the project involves interacting with people in other departments, it requires coordination across the organization. Projects traverse organizational lines because they need skills from multiple departments.

A project usually generates knowledge and skills that become artifacts of organizational value. Senior executives of the organization, including members of human resources, should consider capturing the experiences of the employees involved, especially if team members are planning to leave the organization once the project ends. More importantly, projects have the potential to add to the body of knowledge in the Library and Information Science (LIS) field. What an organization learns during a project can advance the profession for everyone who works in libraries, archives, and museums.

Given that each one is unique, projects involve unfamiliarity and risk. Experts in the project management field estimate that for every US$100 invested in projects worldwide, there is a net loss of $13.50, "lost forever—unrecoverable" (PMI's Pulse, 2013, p. 8). Organizations have something at stake when performing projects. The effort calls for scrutiny because failure could jeopardize the organization. Projects spawn cynics because they require new ways of doing work and have unexpected problems. Furthermore, people in organizational roles build and maintain work that they own and use, while those participating in project work create products that will pass on to someone else.

The risk of failure is highest at the beginning of the project and decreases over time as the project team achieves milestones and provides deliverables. As the effort finishes, the confidence level increases and the success of the project becomes more likely.

Projects consume resources in the form of time, money, materials, and labor. One of the primary missions as a project manager is to serve as the steward of these resources and apply them as sparingly and efficiently as possible.

Project constraints—time, cost, and scope—are inextricably linked. The set of constraints is so universal that it is known by several names, such as the project triangle, the iron triangle, and the triple constraint (Figure 1.1). The triangle is representative of the way a project works: its sides are dependent on each other, just as the three project factors rely on each other as well. A change to one side of the triangle will affect the other sides.

For most projects, one of these three parameters is fixed, but flexibility exists in at least one of the other two. If costs change, then time or scope

Figure 1.1 The Triple Constraint

will need to be modified. The project may have to use less expensive resources, reduce its quality, or cut its schedule. If time is of the essence, the scope or cost will require modification. If the scope changes, then cost or time will need to be amended.

Experienced project managers will know which side of the triangle to modify to receive the desired outcomes. Poor project managers will ask a team to get the project finished on time without additional expenditure. They will be given answers they want to hear, but not the tools to make realistic decisions. This creates internal problems and turmoil, and results in projects that are over budget and delivery dates that slip. Some problems regarding the triple constraint cannot be fixed. It is better to know as soon as possible that a project will be delayed or over budget so that contingency plans can be put in place.

Successful projects do not happen by accident. They are the result of a knowledgeable project manager, a mature project team, and a vision of what the project should achieve. Projects occur whether people manage them or not. Left unattended, projects seem endless and expend resources, but still do not deliver results. Project management makes projects successful.

1.2 WHAT IS PROJECT MANAGEMENT?

Project management has been performed for thousands of years. The monuments of the ancient world, such as Egypt's pyramids, Rome's splendors, and the temple complexes of the Khmer empire, have the hallmarks of modern-day projects. None would have been accomplished without engineering, financing, labor, and management.

Projects of astonishing complexity characterized the late nineteenth century, as nations built skyscrapers, railroads, and ships. By the early twentieth century civil engineers were beginning to think more systematically about their work as they listened to advocates of scientific management. Some of the techniques used by contemporary project managers came into practice. The Hoover Dam made extensive use of a graphic planning tool developed by Henry Laurence Gantt (1861–1919): the now familiar Gantt chart. In World War II a formal project management discipline emerged. During and after the war the US government was engaged in enormous development projects. The Manhattan Project, in which the atomic bomb was designed and built, is recognized as the first endeavor to use modern project management techniques. In the late 1950s

DuPont, aided by the computing technology of Remington Rand Univac, applied critical path methodology to a project that coordinated complex plant operations and maintenance. Around the same time, Booz Allen Hamilton worked with the US Navy to create the project evaluation and review technique (PERT), which was integral to the development of the Polaris nuclear submarine program. These government initiatives required innovation and invention, because existing management techniques were inadequate and modern methods were required.

A project-driven workplace emerged in the 1990s as the discipline of project management extended from the construction and defense industries into corporations, nonprofits, and government agencies. Today, project management has become formalized, and many companies have adopted a management-by-projects approach. Some organizations have established project management offices (PMOs) to assist them in developing standards to manage projects. PMOs maintain and manage projects, as well as ensuring that project management is practiced appropriately throughout the organization. Compared to corporations, libraries, archives, and museums are less likely to have formal PMO offices. In smaller organizations one staff member is devoted to project management or a portion of a full-time employee's responsibilities may be to lead projects.

An increasing demand for project management tools has fueled the development of software, methodologies, and applications to aid project managers in their pursuit of success. Training and certification have been directed toward gaining control over the complexity associated with managing projects. Universities offer master's degrees in the discipline, and some bestow doctorates. Skill sets that were originally developed on an ad hoc basis are now a growing industry.

Project management applies knowledge, techniques, and skills to activities to achieve requirements no matter what the project. It is "organized common sense" (Wysocki, 2011, p. 41). "Whether it's a $50,000 study or a $30 billion 'giga' project, the basic tenets of project management should not change" (Closing, 2009, p. 10). Several methodologies can be employed when managing projects. Two of the more popular methods are the PMBOK (Project Management Body of Knowledge) approach, which is used in North America, and PRINCE2 (PRojects IN Controlled Environments), which is utilized in the United Kingdom. This book will focus on the first methodology, which is supported by the Project Management Institute.

PMBOK project management is accomplished through distinct phases involving the processes of initiating, planning, executing, monitoring, and

Table 1.3 Project Life-Cycle Stages

Stages	Goals	Outputs
Initiating	Authorize the project	Project charter and preliminary project scope statement
Planning	Prepare and schedule the work to perform the project	Project management plan that contains auxiliary plans, such as scope management plan and schedule management plan
Executing	Perform the project work	Project deliverables
Monitoring	Supervise the progress to correct variances from the plan	Change requests for preventive and corrective actions
Closing	Finalize the project	Project acceptance and contract closure

closing. The project life-cycle model describes the stages that projects pass through to their conclusion, as well as their goals and outputs (Table 1.3). Although projects are different, they progress through similar steps.

Initiation authorizes the project, and grants approval to commit resources to working on it. The phase classifies what the project will endeavor to accomplish when it is finished. The organization appoints the project manager during this period. He or she creates the charter, the first piece of project documentation. It describes the project's goals and business justifications, and provides a detailed description of its potential results.

The planning phase identifies the work to be done. Projects have a plan that can be used to measure progress during the endeavor. Since every project is unique, the only way to understand and execute it competently is with a plan. A good plan contains details for estimating the people, money, equipment, and materials necessary to get the job done. Because the plan is the foundation for measuring progress, it acts as a warning system for tasks that are late or over budget. The planning phase develops policies, procedures, and other documentation that define the project. It also involves determining alternative courses of action and selecting from among the best of those to produce the project's goals. Planning has more processes than any other project management phase because it is essential to the operations of the remaining phases.

Execution implements the plan. The project manager coordinates resources to meet the objectives to ensure that the work aligns with the project's goals. Approved changes to the plan are implemented. Sometimes the changes require adjustments to plans or schedules to keep the project on track. During this period the greatest amount of effort and resources are expended to complete project activities. Additionally, the most conflict over schedules will occur in this phase.

Monitoring measures, verifies, and accepts the project's work. Action is taken to correct work that is unaligned with the project plan. Performance measurements are evaluated to determine if variances exist between the work results and the project plan. If corrective action is needed, this may mean another pass through the planning phase to adjust project activities, resources, schedules, and budgets.

After the team completes the project, the closing phase commences. The project team captures what it has learned and finalizes the administrative tasks that end the project. Contract closeout occurs, and the project manager obtains formal acceptance from stakeholders. Unfortunately, closing is often skipped. Once the project is complete, teams tend to jump into the next project. Taking the time to archive project documents will be helpful when you undertake a new project that is similar in size and scope to the project you have completed. You can then review the documents, reuse templates, and save time by evaluating risks and plans to hasten the planning process for the next project.

Throughout the project phases, project management is an attempt to get nonroutine work to flow through the organization, usually horizontally rather than in a vertical, bureaucratic manner. A project management methodology is required to accomplish this workflow because it facilitates the integration of work across various functional units. Not only is the work unique, but organizational systems to complete it are one of a kind as well.

Project management departs from traditional management, also called functional management, where anticipated outcomes are inevitable and fewer parties are involved. Traditional management focuses on operations. This view of management looks at an organization as a set of ongoing activities. In these stable and predictable situations, procedures that rely on centralized decision-making and adherence to hierarchical authority work well. When conditions require adaptability and response to changes, project management achieves better results than traditional management. It provides the specialized technical and managerial competency, decentralized communication, and decision-making necessary to meet the challenges of complex, unfamiliar activities. Project management involves coordinating many actions in a way that is unique to the discipline (Table 1.4).

Table 1.4 Project Management Activities

- Determining goals and objectives
- Working within budgets
- Setting up schedules
- Selecting teams and establishing individual roles
- Communicating progress to stakeholders
- Ensuring the tools, resources, and technology are in place
- Monitoring progress and controlling the project
- Upholding quality standards
- Maintaining team morale
- Dealing with problems that arise
- Completing projects
- Assessing the project's performance

Introducing a new approach to an organization is, above all, a change in its culture. Project management is change management. A structured approach ensures that changes are implemented and their lasting benefits are achieved. It requires different, sensitive, and difficult management tasks compared with the ones that functional managers usually have.

Organizations deliver projects; no single individual or group can do it alone. Project management unites individuals to form a team working toward a common goal. More than any other endeavor, project work is teamwork. People from different organizational areas accomplish projects. Project management harnesses the thoughts and efforts of everyone serving on the team and directs their capabilities toward achieving results.

There must be an agreement among the project stakeholders on the goals of the project. The importance of having clear objectives seems obvious, yet thousands of projects do not have distinct goals, and the results of this ambiguity can be demoralizing.

Management support is necessary because project managers lack the authority to make the decisions required to complete a project. They depend on people in traditional management roles to supply resources, make decisions, and remove obstacles. Even the most enthusiastic, creative, and motivational project managers will be ineffective if they are unable to enlist people with authority in their organizations to act on their behalf. Techniques are used to "manage upward"—that is, to guide the people with power toward making timely decisions that keep the project moving.

Ongoing project status reports enable shifting resources to complete projects that support the organization's top priorities. These reports identify projects that distract from the organization's mission so that they can be stopped before further critical resources are spent.

Project management is fundamentally a decision-making discipline. The decisions we make shape the project's outcomes, but the choices themselves are created by the preferences, priorities, and values of the decision-makers.

Project managers communicate with team members and stakeholders from project conception through to completion. They estimate the effort, cost, and time it will take to deliver a project, and evaluate whether its benefits will justify the costs. They build cohesive teams that are productive even though team members may be new to working together.

Several challenges occur while managing projects, regarding personnel, estimating, and authority. Every project has different staff needs. The number of people required and their diverse skill sets vary for each project. This is compounded in organizations in which several projects occur at the same time. To evaluate potential projects, organizations need accurate cost and schedule estimates, but because each project is unique, estimates may contain more assumptions than facts. When projects cross organizational boundaries, it is no longer clear who has authority for many decisions.

Project management depends on a variety of skill sets that involve the management of scope, time, procurement, human resources, communication, quality, cost, and risk. Each will be discussed briefly.

Scope management defines the work to be performed. It includes project and phase initiations, developing the written scope statement, and listing deliverables. One cause of considerable difficulty for project managers is scope changes. When work is outsourced, scope management also involves ensuring that the vendor completes everything agreed upon in the contract.

Time management includes creating the work breakdown structure, determining dependency relationships among tasks, estimating task efforts and durations, and creating schedules. During the planning process, documents are designed to illustrate how the project tasks will be sequenced. The controlling and monitoring process tracks and reports on the progress of work, as well as adjusting the schedule to address changes in the project plan. Finally, the closing process includes an audit of time targets.

Procurement management involves developing, executing, and monitoring contracts with vendors. It also includes soliciting bids, selecting appropriate vendors, and closing contracts once the project ends. Project managers purchase, license, and lease equipment and services.

Human resource management addresses the people involved in a project. It includes the planning components of determining what skills are needed, defining the participants' roles and responsibilities, and selecting candidates for these tasks. Project managers should have an extraordinary level of people skills to select, evaluate, and motivate team members.

Communication management involves deciding who needs what information, to what level of detail, at what intervals, and in what formats. Communication among everyone working on the project is vital. From concept to completion, project success depends on the ability to come to agreement, coordinate actions, solve problems, and react to changes. These capabilities require good communication as well. Once a communication plan is approved, project managers make sure that the information is gathered and distributed according to the plan.

Quality management defines what represents quality, monitors it, and examines the project outputs to evaluate their conformance to the plan standards. Upholding quality standards throughout the project results in better satisfaction of user requirements. In addition, the costs incurred in assuring quality can be minimized while ensuring project success. Quality controls shape the final product. By holding the project to a high standard of quality, the project manager will produce results of similar worth.

Cost management incorporates identifying, budgeting, and controlling expenses. Both fixed costs, such as equipment and software purchases, and variable costs, such as team members' salaries, are included in the planning and estimating and are then controlled.

Risk management identifies the potential risks, and determines their likelihood and impacts. Contingencies are developed for the highest risks. As the team executes the project, the project manager can use these contingencies to regain control of the project if risks occur.

Traditional project management happens when each project process occurs one after another. Traditional project management works well when a project is familiar, the goals and solutions are easy to identify, the scope and deliverables are lucid, and the technologies or tools are known. For projects like this, you can define the problem to be solved and build a plan for completing it. As a project manager, you execute the project and perform the usual activities to complete the work and achieve the goals.

With some projects you may not know what the solution will be, so you have to decipher it as you perform the project work. This type of project requires a different approach. Agile project management works through iterations to get closer to a successful outcome. It values individuals

Traditional (linear) vs. agile (iterative

and interactions over processes and tools, working software over documentation, collaboration over contract negotiation, and responding to change over following plans (Fowler and Highsmith, 2001). Agile project management methods originated with software development but have been used in other fields. Archives, libraries, and museums may find the model suitable for their organizations if they have "limited staff resources and [are] interested in a development and management framework for innovative projects. However, its acceptance is dependent on organizational culture and [the] nature of application" (Chang, 2010, p. 672).

In the initiating and planning processes you define the goals of the project and build a plan to achieve them. With agile project management you also determine what you are trying to create with each iteration, then develop a plan for the work in that iteration. Execution is often easier in agile projects because they use small teams of highly skilled people who work in the same location. These conditions make it easier to get everyone committed. With agile project management, you monitor and control the project more carefully and communicate more frequently than with traditional project management. Finally, each iteration has a closing process for accepting its specific deliverables. When stakeholders approve of the results, you can finish the other completion activities, such as closing contracts.

In traditional project management the scope never changes but time and cost are variable. In agile project management the scope is the variable, and time and cost are fixed. You determine whether a traditional or an agile approach makes sense during the initiating process of a project, once you know whether your solution is clear. Knowledge of traditional and nontraditional project management allows project managers to apply the appropriate method to their work.

For large projects or organizations that run multiple projects at the same time, project management software is required because it helps track risks, issues, and other data and builds document libraries. It can handle the development of and changes to Gantt charts and network diagrams, including PERT charts and calculations of critical paths. The software automates many project management procedures, such as planning, viewing your progress, recognizing overscheduling for team members, making adjustments, and generating reports. When considering project management software options, keep in mind the work environment, organizational culture, and the number of projects and their complexity.

Software options are available for making project management easier: measure their pros and cons before implementing them (Table 1.5). Project

Table 1.5 Software Options

Software Type	Strengths	Weaknesses
Specialized project management software	• Allows you to make multiple representations of the plan • Calendar facility allows longer-term scheduling • Shows dependencies between tasks • Integrates schedule, budget, and resource plans • Allows automatic calculations of critical path and resource implications	• Occasional project managers may spend more time learning to use the software than using it • Too complex for small projects • Does not readily integrate project work and day-to-day activities
Spreadsheet software	• Widely available • Flexible for smaller projects • Allows automatic calculation of durations and costs using formulae • Graphical representation of tasks	• Requires specialized knowledge to represent complex information • Does not readily integrate project work and day-to-day activities
Graphics packages	• Makes professional-looking representation of the plan • Have multiple options for representing products, tasks, and responsibilities • Project templates available in many packages	• Not universally available, so some stakeholders may not be able to access the plan • Have no automatic interface with diary or financial packages, so schedules and budgets require manual updating when adjustments are made
Datebook and task list software	• Integration between project and day-to-day work • Good at representing the schedule • Widely available • A familiar format for most stakeholders	• Not good at representing critical path, resource plans, or budgets • No automatic tie-in with budgeting software • Does not allow you to show the relationships between tasks graphically

management lends itself to automation. As long as you can put the software to work quickly and do not have to spend excessive time working through its limitations, duties such as schedule control can be quick. For smaller projects, spreadsheets created by Microsoft or Google may be suitable for scheduling. Online programs like Trello offer a free, flexible, and visual way to show project progress. For complex projects, the most popular desktop programs are Microsoft Project and Primavera. For collaboration, Basecamp and Microsoft SharePoint allow you to share files with others, keep track of issues, and manage workflows. Some information professionals managing projects feel that these programs suffice, and robust project management software is too expensive, too unwieldy, and "too 'corporate'" for their needs (Vinopal, 2012, p. 386). Appendix C offers a list of project management, scheduling, and collaborative software programs.

1.3 PROJECT MANAGEMENT BENEFITS

Fundamentally, project management is an operational art. It is a link between strategy and tactics. Project management applies the goals of the project to the tasks to be performed. Unfortunately, as Cervone (2004) states, "Project management is a challenge for many digital library projects because many librarians do not come from a background that accepts and embraces project management concepts" (p. 162). All information professionals share this problem. However, this does not have to be the case, especially when librarians, archivists, and museum professionals understand the benefits of project management and champion its methodologies in their home institutions.

Projects can be completed without project management, but project management increases the odds of successful, cost-effective projects. As Massis (2010) explains:

> Our work in libraries today often involves coordinating projects with numerous tasks and engaging various levels of people assigned to complete the project within a specified time limit and often under very challenging budget constraints. All too often, projects are implemented without proper planning and then, when they do not work out as planned or fail completely, the stakeholders are left to explain what happened and why. If more libraries adopted the methodology of project management, the likelihood of project failure might well decrease considerably (p. 526).

Project management requires time and energy, but it rewards organizations with control, documentation, and focused labor. Project management benefits include better scheduling, improved estimating, higher levels of quality, earlier identification of problems, and more efficient measurements of success than working without a project management methodology. Shorter development times, lower costs, and higher worker morale are additional advantages.

Dojka (1990) credits project management for the success in founding the Yale University Archives, specifically:

> the development of concrete plans, goals, and timelines; flexibility in tactics used to achieve goals; the commitment of working with and through existing programs and structures whenever possible; and a keen awareness of the importance of interpersonal skills (p. 560).

Organizations turn to project management to meet demands. They employ project management methodologies to deliver what their patrons want without exhausting the people who make it happen. Institutions can become more innovative, productive, and responsive, and see improvements in their operations. Most importantly, they will have faster returns on their investment. Delivering projects on schedule and within budget constraints means that patrons receive services more quickly. Support of strategic goals is also possible because project management focuses on why a project is important and what it is trying to achieve.

Project management allows for flexibility. With efficient management, teams can analyze the effect of changes that arise throughout the project life cycle and develop alternatives swiftly. Project management also increases productivity. Applying measures means that people complete their work and are ready to move on to the next assignment quicker.

Good project management makes labor a success. Conversely, poor project management nullifies the efforts of talented people. Although no project manager can make mediocre work spectacular, excellent efforts can be overlooked if the project management required to deliver the project is absent.

A project management methodology also creates more stakeholder buy-in within institutions conducting projects. Afshari and Jones (2007) write about developing an institutional repository at the Imperial College London library using the PRINCE2 methodology that the college requires for all new projects. Employing a recognized approach "put the repository team in an excellent position having both top-down and bottom-up support for the endeavour," as well as the skill sets to achieve the project (p. 341).

Project management adds value by reducing unreasonable deadlines and budgets and making estimating easier and more accurate. It promotes best practices across projects while eliminating the repetitions of known errors, giving stakeholders precise information about the project status and the prospects for completion. It ensures that the right projects are done in the right way. Good project management increases the probability that a project will thrive; and when a project succeeds, everyone with a stake in it benefits.

Project management estimates the effort, cost, and time it will take to deliver a project and evaluates whether its benefits will justify the forecasted costs. It coordinates the actions of a diverse workforce, assembled specifically for a project, to achieve the goal within cost and time constraints. It accounts for progress and productivity to provide accurate forecasts of completion dates and budget amounts.

Project management optimizes results by striking the right balance between scope, cost, schedule, and quality. It focuses projects on the business objectives and strategy of the organization. It makes optimal use of resources, including expertise, and provides useful information for making decisions. Project management promotes creativity and innovation by creating an environment of openness and visibility underlined by the importance of communication. *Current sources cited!*

In a paper discussing a project in which the University of Edinburgh added its library, archival, and museum collections to the information management application ArchivesSpace, Hosker et al. (2015) state:

> The overarching project management provided the core structure for project focus and movement to free up the creativity and technical skills of [archivists and collections staff] to work together to achieve platforms of authoritative linked data about the collections (p. 159).

In this instance, project management allowed the university to perform a cultural shift in how it linked, managed, and made available its heritage data.

In addition to providing value to organizations, project management offers significance to project managers and individuals in the project team. Project management ensures that organizations recognize everyone's work and apply it to its best use. It provides a career path that offers challenging opportunities for each new project. It can often be a stepping stone for promotion. There is also significant freedom of choice and variety for project managers, as no two days of a project are alike. Using project management skills builds on professional abilities and knowledge, including management, soft skills, and technical expertise. Project management provides a strong sense of accomplishment, and affords the opportunity to effect change across the organization. It prepares individuals for leadership positions and allows them to be on the front lines of strategic initiatives.

Project management requires action to create the conditions for success and put in place the strategies and structures to direct the dynamic nature of project work. Working smarter on projects will undoubtedly enable libraries, archives, and museums to meet whatever challenges that may come their way.

CHAPTER 2

Selection and Prioritization

Knowing is not enough, we must apply. Willing is not enough, we must do.

Johann Wolfgang von Goethe

It does not take much strength to do things, but it requires a great deal of strength to decide what to do.

Elbert Hubbard

I keep six honest serving-men

(They taught me all I knew);

Their names are What and Why and When

And How and Where and Who.

Rudyard Kipling

2.1 IDENTIFYING THE PROJECT

The most vital aspect of managing a successful project is identifying the right problem to be solved. Project managers should deliver projects that add value to the organization. Projects should reduce costs, expand services, or increase efficiency. Projects that are properly defined and executed should be linked to these objectives from start to finish. Project managers must change their mindsets from simply completing the project to strategically implementing the project with business objectives in mind.

Every project that is being considered should also withstand some essential questions (Table 2.1). The proposed project should align with the organization's strategic goals and priorities. If it fails to do so, the effort may waste time and resources that should have been applied to more important organizational priorities. Activities that identify, analyze, and improve existing processes are often excellent candidates for projects (Table 2.2). Process measures examine the efficiency of daily procedures that use resources, primarily staff time. These are common in information centers like libraries, archives, and museums, where value-added services and experiences are appreciated. Consider project suitability as well (Table 2.3). The right projects satisfy three simple but necessary criteria: they address an

Project Management for Information Professionals
ISBN 978-0-08-100127-1

Table 2.1 Essential Project Questions

- What is the problem we are trying to solve?
- How are we going to solve the problem?
- What is our plan?
- How will we know when we are done?
- How well did the project go?

Table 2.2 Possible Process Improvement Projects

- Improving conditions or decisions
- Improving flow of processes
- Reducing bottlenecks
- Reducing backlogs
- Eliminating activities that lack business value
- Reducing or eliminating errors
- Reducing or eliminating frustration
- Reducing or eliminating waste
- Improving process quality, especially minimizing rework
- Implementing concurrent processes

Table 2.3 Project Suitability Questions

- Does the project solve a problem?
- Is the problem worthy of being solved?
- Is this the right time to do the project?
- Is the project innovative?
- Are there measurable cost or performance benefits?
- Will user satisfaction be positively affected?
- Does the project contribute to our organizational mission?
- Does the project contribute to the current goals of the organization?
- Does the project have significant support within our organization?
- Do we have the time to oversee this project?
- Can our organization handle the additional work caused by this project?
- Does our organization have the funds necessary to support the project?
- Will the project need less money to continue than to start?
- Is the project worth the effort for our organization?
- Who will be influenced by the project?
- What are the risks of project failure?

established need; they are shown to be worthwhile financial investments; and they rank among the best opportunities. Many projects are good ideas, but organizations should only implement the best and most appropriate projects with the greatest impact.

Explore potential projects by creating a business case for them, analyzing the many opportunities they could provide the organization (Table 2.4). The business case is a justification for a proposed project based on its expected benefits. It describes success in terms of measurable positive results. It includes the issues to be addressed, the goals for undertaking such a project, and the project's objectives. It also explores scope, risks, the cost-benefit analysis, and the return on investment (ROI).

The sponsor is often the best person to develop the business case because he or she will handle delivering a successful outcome. Project managers may help to develop business cases as well, because this allows them to become

Table 2.4 Business Case Considerations

Opportunity	Problem
Strategic fit	How will the project contribute to the organization's strategic direction?
Interdependencies	How will this project affect or be affected by other projects?
Success criteria	What measures describe a successful project outcome?
Options considered	What are the alternatives to the chosen solution?
Risks	What are the project's challenges?
Benefits	What are the project's merits?
Costs	What are the comprehensive expenses?
Cost-benefit analysis	Will the benefits outweigh the costs, and by how much?
Deliverables and timescales	What are the deliverables and their due dates?
Planning assumptions	What assumptions have been made?
Benefits realization plan	How will the benefits be measured and delivered?
Management by objectives	What incentives will be offered to promote a successful outcome?

familiar with the project they will run. It is also necessary for them to be involved in the business case since it will secure the needed project resources. Senior executives should approve the business case once it is completed. A business case should show anticipated expenditures versus savings, cost-benefit ratios, and the expected business impact on the organization.

A SWOT analysis, a review of the internal and external environments to determine the strengths, weaknesses, opportunities, and threats, is helpful for determining the business case. Strengths and weaknesses are environmental factors internal to the organization; opportunities and threats address external issues. The analysis is a classic tool used in strategic planning and capital budgeting. At the project level, it provides a rationale for the project, or it may uncover information that matches the organization's resources and capabilities to the environment in which it operates. A template may be found in Appendix E.

Another similar assessment technique is the PEST (political, economic, social, and technological) analysis, or the extended version PESTEL, which adds environmental and legislative aspects. The procedure is helpful when conducting a strategic analysis of macro-environmental factors that an organization needs to take into consideration when selecting projects.

If the project is large or innovative, a feasibility study may be required before beginning the detailed work of planning and implementation. A feasibility study takes into account the variables of the project, including budget, resources, and time constraints, and determines the likelihood of completion given the available resources. It aids you in determining the validity of a proposed project or a section of the project. You may also be tasked with writing a feasibility study to examine the fiscal aspects of the project. If a project can be done in many ways, a feasibility study can clarify the best option to achieve the objectives. It can also help determine if the project is unachievable.

Feasibility studies are written with upper management in mind. As you draft it, explore how the proposed project will benefit the organization. The study usually includes an executive summary, the purpose, the business opportunity, a description of the options assessed, assumptions, the potential audience, financial obligations, and recommended actions. Each section should be brief and provide references to historical information and supporting evidence.

For large projects, you may need to present the costs and benefits in the form of a cost-benefit analysis. It determines if the benefits offset the costs, if the payback period is acceptable, and if the project is worth doing. Performing a cost-benefit analysis may involve some mathematical adjustment to reflect the effects of inflation and the change in the value of costs over time.

Organizations often rely on financial calculations as a comparative tool and an aid for executive approval of projects. The cost-benefit analysis includes a combination of four metrics: net present value (NPV), internal rate of return (IRR), payback period, and cash hole.

Calculating a project's NPV determines how much money the project will make or save. It is a calculation in dollars of the present value of future cash flows expected from a project, and is roughly analogous to the concept of profit. It evaluates the monies returned on a project for each period the project lasts. For example, a project may last three years, but there may be a ROI in each of the three years the project is in existence, not just at the end of the project. Appraising the IRR defines how rapidly the money will be returned. It is a calculation of the percentage rate at which the project will yield wealth. It is comparable to the effective yield of a savings account. Gauging the payback period examines when the project's benefits will recover the amount spent. It is expressed in months or years. Calculating the cash hole, also known as maximum exposure, determines how much has been invested at any given point in time. It answers the question: "What is the most the organization has invested in any given point in time?" The cash hole is expressed in terms of dollars.

Project managers should recognize the authority, political standing, and aspirations of senior executives during the project selection phase. Powerful stakeholders are likely to get their projects approved based on who they are. While business cases and feasibility studies enlighten some stakeholders, if an executive in the organization champions a project and has enough influence to get it approved, there may be little choice except to implement it. In this case, as project manager you can apply processes to make the project as helpful as possible given the circumstances.

A proposal is the first step to launching a project. It includes the vision of the project that the stakeholders authorized for completion. The proposal is a necessary fiction because it is an idealized version of what the project could be. It is impossible to know for certain what future steps and technologies will be appropriate to complete any deliverables. In transforming the proposal into a plan, one needs to be flexible. The pace of change in technology means that once the work begins, there may be better means to do the tasks. However, the project proposal contains both the intellectual vision for the work and a plan for its completion.

2.2 DETERMINING GOALS AND OBJECTIVES

Goals describe the purpose of the project, while objectives express the steps that are necessary to achieve goals. The goals should be prioritized, so the team knows which goal is most important in the event that a trade-off needs to be made. Document each goal and tie it to the project vision. Goals describe what you want to achieve in nontechnical terms, and should align with organizational strategy. They define the outcome of the project in clear terms so that everyone understands what is to be accomplished.

A goal statement is a point of reference for any questions that arise regarding the project's scope or purpose. The sponsor and project manager must set expectations and encourage the refinement of the goals so that the team gains ownership of the project, builds cooperation, and reduces areas of conflict. Organizations may divide their goals into three broad categories: "service goals, resource management goals, and administrative/directional goals" (Johnson, 1994, p. 9).

A goal should be presented in such a way that one can determine if it has been achieved. If the goal of the project is to produce a deliverable with a specified quality at a particular time and within a cost limit, it is easy to check if the goal is achieved.

Goal statements should be short and to the point. They should be devoid of any language or terminology that could confuse anyone reading them. The goals should exclude any information that might commit the project to dates or deliverables that are impractical. Remember that you lack much detail about the project at this time.

Goals need to be translated into objectives if they are to be used for planning and guiding the project's assessment. Objectives should define what is to be achieved, when it will be completed, and how it will be performed. Objectives are a more detailed version of the goal statements. The purpose of objective statements is to clarify the boundaries of the goals and define the scope of your project. Objectives specify a future state, rather than an activity.

Objectives are statements that tell the project team what result is to be achieved. Problem-solving to determine methods to reach objectives should be kept open so that solutions can be determined later. If the

Examples of good and bad goals &

approach is written into the objectives, it may lock a team into a method that may be unsuitable for the project. *objectives would be helpful*

Objectives document the project's critical success factors, which are statements of qualitative criteria describing what will make the project work. You must specify what needs to be done, when it should be done, and what measures will be used to evaluate success.

Objectives range widely. Financial objectives refer to the budgets themselves, or to the standards organizations employ to assess their performance. Examples of financial objectives include achieving a ROI, staying within budget, increasing revenue or profit, and cutting costs. Performance objectives include meeting deadlines, satisfying requirements, and conforming to specifications. Technical objectives relate to the implementation or improvement of technology. Quality objectives represent improvements in services.

Use the word SMART (specific, measurable, accurate, realistic, and timebound) to remind yourself of the areas to consider when setting objectives. Specific objectives tell exactly what, where, and how to address a need. Measurable objectives have metrics in place so you know whether you have succeeded or not. Accurate objectives should be described in a precise manner, so errors are nonexistent. Realistic objectives should be able to be achieved in the time allowed. Timebound objectives must include a precise date for achievement. You may also consider writing SMARTER objectives, adding extending and rewarding. The objectives should stretch or extend the capabilities of the organization. Rewarding objectives may be more difficult to gauge, but the achievement of an objective that serves the parent body will often translate into greater support for the organization and the project in the future.

State objectives explicitly to avoid confusion. A comparison of good and bad objectives demonstrates the effectiveness of soundly crafted objectives (Table 2.5). Their differences can influence the success of the project.

As in planning, the process of developing objectives is continuous. As information becomes available, and as the project progresses, modifications will need to be made to the objectives that contribute to the achievement of the completed project. In the planning phase the project is in flux, so you can revise your objectives later as you receive more information.

Prioritizing objectives may help eliminate tasks if the commitment to your budget or completing the project on time becomes an issue. Priorities will also assist you if you need to reorganize the project or deploy team

Table 2.5 Comparison of Good and Bad Objectives

Good Objectives	Bad Objectives
Stated in terms of concrete end results	Stated in terms of activities, deliverables, features, or processes
Each limited to a single significant result	More than one objective in the statement
Clearly stated	Compound or too broad
Achievable in a stated period	Never fully achievable in a stated period
Related to the outcome of the project	Ambiguous in defining what is expected
Critical to the success of the project	Not of real consequence
Precisely stated in terms of quantities	Too brief, long, or complex
Definite measurement standards and methods	Theoretical, idealistic, or impractical
Formally documented	Undocumented
A mix of short- and long-term objectives	Either all short- or all long-term objectives
Unique	Restatements of other objectives

members. If two people are completing a task and assistance with another task associated with a higher priority objective is required, you will be able to adjust their efforts to be the most useful.

2.3 FORMULATING STRATEGIES

It is worth taking a moment to think about how the project could be transformed from delivering a suitable solution to being a project that catches the imagination of those in the Library and Information Science field. This should only take a short amount of time; just suspend judgment on ideas and be creative. Try to identify more than one option, even when there is an obvious solution. Take the time to consider at least three possible approaches. The goal should be to find one way to make your project exciting and different for your organization as well as for the communities you serve.

Once you know the goal and objectives of the project, you will find many approaches from which to choose. Brainstorming can generate ideas for projects and how to go about achieving them (Table 2.6).

Table 2.6 Brainstorming Tips

- Create an atmosphere of enthusiasm, engagement, and originality.
- Stress the quantity of ideas over quality.
- List all ideas offered by team members; unusual ideas are welcome.
- Ask every member of the group to contribute their ideas.
- Focus on creativity rather than criticism.
- Discuss ideas only to clarify understanding.
- Encourage ambitious ideas. They can be assessed at a later date.
- Support the creation of many ideas. The more ideas generated, the greater the chance of finding a useful one.
- When the brainstorming ebbs, pause for a while and start again.
- Combine or modify ideas already identified.

A small group should read the problem statement, the goals, and the objectives, and begin generating strategies. Provide paper to team members and encourage them to document as many ideas as they can on their own. Capture each idea on a separate piece of paper. When everyone finishes, ask each person to read his or her ideas aloud and write each idea where it is visible to the group. Continue until you have accumulated the ideas in a list. Include new suggestions generated while listening to others' submissions. The team should focus on collecting options as quickly as possible without criticism. If some ideas are similar, work to consolidate them. If ideas seem analogous, but the people who contributed them think they are different, leave them listed separately.

Once you have some strategies written down, start evaluating them. The group should determine how well the approach satisfies the project objectives. You could discuss ideas further to generate information on costs and benefits or apply decision-making using weighted criteria. Another method is to have each person rank the ideas on the list and then consolidate the rankings to define the overall prioritization.

The strategy with the highest rating is most likely your winner. The group should discuss the feasibility of the approach. Methods that utilize unproven methods or new technologies might be unfeasible. The project team should consider the risks of the stratagem. You can execute an initial risk analysis to evaluate whether any risks are significant enough that you will want to stop the project. Additionally, the approach should fit the culture of the organization. Forcing a tactic that is alien to organizational culture is fighting a losing battle.

The strategy you choose should satisfy most, if not all, of the project objectives. Once you select a strategy, the details of your project will begin to become apparent.

2.4 GATHERING REQUIREMENTS

Requirements are dissimilar to goals and objectives. Requirements are definitions of what the deliverables of the project must be once the project is completed. They define the final product, service, or result. These are statements of quantitative criteria, each of which provides a measure of one or more of the project's critical success factors. You can visualize requirements if you consider the current condition of an organization and then examine the future state of the institution after the project is completed.

As a project manager you may handle gathering the requirements, though this responsibility often rests with the business analyst. It is helpful for you to understand the process techniques and outputs of collecting requirements so that you can form a complete picture of how the project is defined and what the stakeholders are anticipating from it.

Requirements should be detailed and specific, and vary in type and intention (Table 2.7). They must have several conditions to be part of a successful project (Table 2.8). Keep two components in mind as you determine requirements: gathering the correct information, and translating it into workable requirements with measurable deliverables.

Requirements may start out broadly, but as the collection process evolves they will be reduced into smaller requirements. At that level, requirements tend to be interrelated. For example, a high-priority requirement may be dependent upon a lower-priority one. Requirements also necessitate documentation at the start of the project so that, throughout the project, the fulfillment of the requirements can be gauged.

Table 2.7 Requirement Types and Intentions

Type	Intention
External	Requirements from outside the organization to which the project must adhere
Functional	Requirements relating to the performance of the project result
Operational	Requirements concerning the use of the project result
Design	Requirements pertaining to the realization of the project result

Could be illustrated with more vivid examples from cultural heritage institutions

Table 2.8 Requirement Conditions

- Complete: Requirements define constraints, assumptions, and risks. There is enough accurate information that the team may create the requirements based on the documentation provided.
- Consistent: Requirements should complement other project requirements.
- Correct: Requirements should describe the functionality accurately.
- Feasible: Requirements should be possible to implement based on the resources, schedule, cost, quality, and risks.
- Modifiable: Similar requirements should be grouped together so that changes can be made. When requirements are grouped, it is easy to see how a change in one requirement affects other requirements.
- Necessary: Requirements should have value and contribute to meeting goals and objectives as stated in the project charter.
- Testable: Each requirement must be verified upon delivery by testing to confirm their completeness.
- Unambiguous: The requirements documentation should be written in clear, concise language so readers arrive at the same understanding of what the requirements demand.

Table 2.9 MoSCoW Analysis

- Must: These requirements must be implemented for the solution to be deemed a success.
- Should: These requirements should be implemented in the solution, but are unnecessary for the solution's success.
- Could: These requirements would be nice to include in the solution if possible, but they are not the most important of the requirements.
- Will not: These requirements have been identified but are not going to be implemented in the project solution due to cost, complexity, timing, or any number of other reasons. These requirements may be implemented in the solution later.

Stakeholders often combine wish-list items with conditions. Sometimes people who are not stakeholders append their requirements to your project. As the project manager, you must distinguish between essential, desirable, and unnecessary requirements. Essential requirements are what the project must deliver. Desirable requirements are included in the scope but could be dropped without damaging the project. Unnecessary requirements can be excluded without impact on the project. One approach you can use to prioritize the requirements is the MoSCoW analysis, which places each requirement into one of four categories (Table 2.9).

To prioritize your requirements you will need to decide, with the assistance of your stakeholders, which are must-haves, good-to-haves, and like-to-haves. Requirement prioritization is a consultative process, with the stakeholders making the final decision.

Consider reusing existing requirements. If you are working on a project similar to one performed in the past, you can use existing requirements as a foundation for your current project. This approach reduces duplicated effort, and you may be able to improve on the previous solution based on past feedback.

For software applications, creating a prototype can encourage creative ideas and help users explain what they need. A prototype is a rough model used to test an idea. Built early in the development phase of the project, it provides insight into how an application will look, feel, and work. Prototypes are used to gather and document requirements, and, after feedback, gain additional requirements.

The prototype, or even a rough draft of the requirements, can act as a straw man for stakeholders to critique. Users can use the draft as a tool to articulate their needs better. By stating what they do not need, stakeholders show what they are seeking in the project.

Project managers and business analysts can use several elicitation techniques to gather requirements (Table 2.10). These methods, which range from document analysis to in-depth interviews, provide some ideas for needed projects. Interviewing users can help identify the processes they use and the functions they require. A structured approach helps provide the necessary information. For example, a first series of interviews could document initial requirements, while a second round could review and refine them.

Surveys and questionnaires can provide useful information to help you gather your requirements. You need to design the questionnaire carefully and determine if you want to ask open- or closed-ended questions. A challenge is making sure you are not leading people's responses, but allowing them to tell you what is important to them.

If your project involves several departments, hold meetings with representatives from each faction to discuss their needs. These meetings not only identify necessities, but also assist in obtaining buy-in from the departments that attend. You may want to hold separate meetings for different audiences, such as the reference team and the IT department.

There are also elicitation tools for gathering requirements from existing materials, such as document analysis, interface analysis, and reverse

Table 2.10 Elicitation Techniques

- Comparative analysis: Be alert to the way in which other organizations are being innovative.
- Document analysis: Study existing documentation to determine the questions to ask.
- Focus groups: Hold a gathering of five to 10 people to solicit their suggestions and assess requirements.
- Forecasting: Focus on trend analysis as a basis for predicting future needs and expectations.
- Interface analysis: Examine interfaces with your technical stakeholders to understand how the system interacts with other systems, hardware, and users.
- Interviews: Ask questions of your interviewees and use the answers to shape your requirements.
- Observation: Watch users perform their tasks to get an insight into an organization's operations.
- Prototyping: Develop a model of the project so users can envision what the solution will look like.
- Requirements workshops: Also called facilitated work sessions or joint application development sessions, this technique gathers team members in highly structured meetings.
- Reverse engineering: See how a product is built by taking it apart. With software, this approach means examining the code.
- Surveys: Use these appraisals to elicit requirements from stakeholders and understand user needs or desires.

engineering. These techniques are not meant to stand alone, but should be combined in a way that is most useful for your project. They should also be iterated: you will never receive all the information at once. You may begin with a critical mass of data to start analyzing and determining the requirements, then need to return to your stakeholders to get more information to clarify and expand upon your findings.

As the project evolves you may discover there are implied requirements that were never documented. You may also find unfeasible requirements given the existing project parameters. Additionally, extraneous requirements may be identified. Changes to the project are discussed in Chapter 5.

The requirements baseline is the standard agreement that pending change requests are measured against in the project. Its purpose is to detect defects and poor quality, as well as the small, undocumented changes to the project scope called scope creep. When stakeholders sign off on the requirements scope, they agree that these identified needs will serve as the baseline for the project, and these items are demanded for the project to be accepted.

2.5 DETERMINING DELIVERABLES

Deliverables are the defined products, results, or services produced and handed over during the project. They include physical properties, documents or other written artifacts, technical features, and acceptable criteria. Identifying deliverables provides a focus to help you ensure that the project is planned to achieve all the results expected of it. Deliverables help define the boundaries of the project scope during the planning process. They can be outputs or outcomes. Outputs have an identifiable product, while outcomes are a changed state that might not be evident for some time.

Develop deliverables by looking at each objective and deciding what is being produced by that objective. The combined lists from each objective inventory the deliverables of the entire project.

It is incumbent upon you as a project manager to ensure that you are working toward the right deliverables. No confusion should exist about deliverables. What if the user has a different idea in mind than you do? Document the deliverable as you understand it relative to its purpose, composition, and quality criteria, and then ask your stakeholders for feedback.

There are two categories of deliverables. Intermediary deliverables are created to be used in subsequent portions of the project. Final deliverables are produced at the end of a project. If a project has many intermediary deliverables, it is better to list the major deliverables in the project plan to enable others to concentrate on these.

Deliverables can be milestones. Milestones mark a significant event, usually the completion of a project phase, a decision point, or the attainment of a major deliverable. They are not activities; they do not take time or consume resources. They are both a state to be achieved and the conditions necessary to attain the state. They act as points in a schedule that indicate a time by which the team should complete critical activities. Because milestones are moments in time, they lack duration in the schedule. Often they have "must be done by" dates and task successors that may affect the successors' schedule. This is discussed further in Chapter 4. Milestones often summarize important events in a project, and help stakeholders keep track of the project when it is unnecessary for them to know every detail. Use milestones to mark a point in time to monitor critical portions of the project. Milestones give team members a deadline to work toward and break a large project into more easily completed phases.

2.6 CLARIFYING SUCCESS CRITERIA

It is difficult to judge the success of a project until there has been an impression outside the organization. Often people have an easier time finding fault with something than they do in noting positive achievements. Success is sometimes hard for team members and stakeholders to grasp, especially when they are implementing the project.

Success criteria specify how the project is executed. Projects have universal success criteria that include finishing on schedule, keeping costs within budget, and meeting the goals that have been agreed upon by the project stakeholders and team. Additionally, deliverables and objectives are sometimes referred to as critical success factors. They are elements that must be completed for the project to be considered finished.

It is vital to determine critical parameters such as targets, limits, and thresholds. For instance, what is the delivery date? What amount of deadline extension can be tolerated? When do delays dictate that continuation of the effort should be evaluated? Milestone dates help to identify poor conditions early in the project. Target values should also be established for costs, technological accomplishments, and areas where performance is critical to supporting the criteria associated with the original goals. This process is central to prevent wishful-thinking projects from sapping the resources of the organization.

Success criteria such as increased revenue and reduced costs should be measured in hard dollars or as a percentage of a specific revenue number. Improved services in libraries, archives, and museums are an important success criterion, but may be harder to define than financial benefits. They are usually judged by some percentage of improvement in user satisfaction or a reduction in the frequency or type of user complaints.

However, project success is more than just completing the project within the triple constraint of time, cost, and scope. Success depends on a systems approach where project parts are interrelated and managed with an understanding that failure in one area will affect other areas of the project. Success can be displayed by agreement among the team and the stakeholders on the goals of the project, support from management to supply the resources and remove obstacles, and ongoing project communication.

Project efficiency is another level of success to consider. How well was the project managed? If a project meets its targets but the experience adversely affected those involved in it, stakeholders and the team will not perceive the project as successful.

Another factor is utility. To what extent did the project fulfill its mission of solving a problem, exploiting an opportunity, or otherwise satisfying a need? Was the issue resolved? Are users and stakeholders happy? Have the desired results been achieved?

The final aspect to consider is organizational improvement. Did the organization learn from the project? Is that knowledge going to increase the chances that future projects will succeed? High-performing organizations learn from their failures and their successes, and use that knowledge to develop their success rate over time. This meta-level of success assumes a long-term perspective and measures organizational learning and a resultant increase in project accomplishment.

2.7 FORMULATING THE SCOPE STATEMENT

The basis on which successful projects are built is a clear understanding of the scope. Without this, a project manager will struggle to deliver a project well. The scoping stage identifies the size and shape of the project and describes it in a way that helps everyone concerned comprehend its intentions. The project scope is all of the work, and only the required work, which must be completed for the project to be done. A scope statement template may be found in Appendix E. Ask yourself questions to determine the scope of the project (Table 2.11). Scoping is essentially about deciding what lies inside and outside the range of the project; it defines the project's boundaries. The statement is a macro view of what the project will do and what to anticipate when the it is complete. It is sometimes called a statement of work, and is often included in a legal agreement if the project involves hiring a vendor to complete the work.

The purpose of creating a scope statement at the beginning of the project is to have a starting place on which to base future decisions. An unambiguous scope statement helps prevent a project from expanding beyond its boundaries. By communicating the scope statement to the team, you help keep them focused on the tasks to be completed and discourage people from doing unnecessary work.

Some organizations lack a separate scope statement. Instead, project objectives and deliverables determine when something is within scope. However, taking the time to develop a succinct statement of the scope will help everyone in due course, especially when evaluating whether later changes are within scope.

Table 2.11 Scoping Questions

- What are the objectives of the project?
- What is the problem to be solved?
- What would be the repercussions of not fixing it?
- What is the result required?
- What has been tried before?
- Why is this result required?
- Why does it not exist already?
- What are the deliverables?
- Where will the deliverables be used? In what context will they be used?
- Where is the project in the organization's list of priorities?
- How will the quality of deliverables be determined?
- How are users going to measure success at the end of the project?
- Are there constraints on the project?
- Are there currently known issues, risks, or opportunities?
- Are there external considerations?
- Do the stakeholders or users have any implicit requirements, assumptions, or needs that are not defined in the scope documents?
- When will the project deliverables be used?
- Who are the users?
- Who will support it?
- Who will manage it?

The scope statement should give senior management an overview of what to expect throughout the life of the project and what its desired outcome will be. The statement has several components (Table 2.12). It includes the project's context, needs that it is trying to meet, and the outcome in terms of how the organization will adopt the results and how its output will be measured. The statement should include the functions of the project, user and interface needs, quantitative performance and reliability requirements, documentation, training, support, and any other postdelivery needs. Project managers should identify the people who will provide input into the scope of the project, such as senior executives, as well as those who have political power in the organization.

Equally important is a statement of scope exclusions. Stating the omissions enables you to discuss them and add them to the project, if necessary, before any estimates are given. Write the scope exclusions in a separate section of the project plan or a portion of the scope statement.

At the planning stage of the process, the project team can only describe what is known at the time. The scope statement then becomes part of the project charter. Further planning steps will elaborate on this initial scope

Table 2.12 Scope Statement Components

- Objectives
- Scope description
- Deliverables
- Requirements
- Boundaries
- Acceptance criteria
- Constraints
- Assumptions
- Project organization
- Risks
- Schedule milestones
- Fund limitations
- Cost estimates
- Project configuration management requirements
- Project specifications
- Approval requirements

---

statement, providing additional details for estimating, assigning, controlling, and accepting the project deliverables.

At the scoping stage, consider whether the project is worth doing. If it is unlikely to contribute to improvements or add value to the organization, moving forward with it may be pointless. If the project proves to be neither useful nor viable, it is better to discover this before more time and resources are invested.

2.8 CONSIDERING ASSUMPTIONS AND RISKS

Project planning is incomplete until an analysis is made of project risks and their potential impacts. Assessing and managing risks are necessary to guard against catastrophes. Every project has obstacles that could affect its success. Similarly, projects have assumptions that need to be explicated so that the decision-makers know what they are approving.

Risk refers to circumstances that exist outside the project team's control and will have an undesirable impact on the project if they occur. Successful projects ensue when the team addresses potential problems before they happen. Risk management increases the likelihood of success. A reactive project manager attempts to resolve issues when they occur, but a proactive project manager tries to determine problems beforehand. The team may not foretell all problems, and some problems that seem unlikely to transpire

Table 2.13 Areas of Risk

Area	Description
Administrative	Processes, procedures, and changes in roles and responsibilities
Cost	Projected costs, manufacturing or maintenance costs, inflation, currency exchange, and budget limitations
Human	Human error, poor performance, communication complications, and personality conflicts
Labor resources	Quality, quantity, skills, availability, and difficulty in defining roles and responsibilities
Logistical	Inability to deliver materials or work
Marketability	User expectations, pricing, share, demographics, quality, geography, and economy
Organizational	Organizational culture, change in management or priorities, coordination among departments, and office politics
Outside factors	Competitor actions or reactions, and regulations
Scope	Estimated extent of the work, ability to define work clearly, design errors and omissions, and user-driven scope change
Technology	User expectations, probability of success, ability to scale up, product manufacturability, and design success
Time	Project duration, activity duration, time to market, launch date, and timing of management reviews and approvals

may occur. Projects have areas of high uncertainty that may result in risk (Table 2.13).

Brainstorming sessions can identify risks in the project and minimize their impact. A power in numbers exists, since no single person can foresee the dozens of things that could go wrong in a project, especially a large or complex one. As you brainstorm, develop a list of serious risks, then unify similar ones into manageable groups. Once you understand the sources of risk, you will be in a better position to avoid them.

There are several responses to dealing with risk (Table 2.14). One way to approach risks is to list them and describe their probability and impact on the project. Prioritize the risks and determine which ones may need further action. You can then create a response plan, depending on the circumstances. Avoidance refers to activities that circumvent the risk entirely. Plans can be changed so the risk will not happen. Mitigation reduces the

Table 2.14 Risk Responses

- Avoidance: Circumvent the risk. Changes done early in the project will have fewer consequences than later changes later.
- Planned contingency: Have an alternative plan that will achieve the same result by a different route.
- Reduction: Take action to reduce the likelihood or effect of the risk.
- Transference: See if the risk can be moved elsewhere so that the consequences become less severe. The risk does not go away, but becomes someone else's problem. There is usually a fee for transference, and examples include insurance, warranties, guarantees, and fixed-priced contracts with vendors.
- Prevention: Terminate the risk by doing things differently. This is not always a realistic possibility.
- Acceptance: Acquiesce to the risks because other actions are unfeasible or because the risks are small and a formal response is unwarranted.

probability or impact of the risk. It makes the likelihood of the event less severe; depending on the risk itself, one or more mitigations may be available. A standard risk mitigation technique, especially in large, complex projects, is the purchase of insurance to cover costs if an event occurs. On small projects you would rarely purchase insurance, but you could use budget reserves against cost overruns. Transference reassigns the risk to someone else. Another approach is active acceptance, in which the risk is recognized but a contingency plan or budget is developed to deal with it if it happens. Passive acceptance means realizing that there is a risk, but deciding what to do about it only when it occurs.

It is possible to reduce the effect or likelihood of a risk. The specific mitigation may affect either the impact or the probability, or both, so it is important to know what the outcome should be. For instance, if the only person able to produce a significant aspect of the project is a new employee, the possibility of creating a poor-quality deliverable might be lessened by setting expectations at the outset. Requiring the team member to show his or her work halfway through may mitigate the risk because any quality concerns can be addressed.

The likelihood of a risk should be monitored to determine whether it is becoming an issue. For example, if there is a risk that time will run out before completion of user acceptance testing, the likelihood can be monitored by tracking the number of defects being recorded every day. If the number rises, so will the probability of the risk becoming an issue. If the number falls, the probability lessens.

Assumptions are often a critical factor in determining a project's fate. Projects rest on assumptions, whether or not they are acknowledged or verified. Every person makes assumptions, but we seldom realize this or analyze them. Listing assumptions can be one of the most difficult sections of the plan to complete. Often we assume many things throughout the course of a project, but continuous conversation will make sure that we do not keep our presuppositions for long. You do not know what you are assuming, so it is important that communication continues to determine what these assumptions are and you come to a consensus about their resolution.

Try to recognize when you and your team members are making assumptions, and take the time to identify, examine, and validate what you implicitly assume. List the major assumptions that can impact the project's success if they turn out to be untrue. As with objectives, each project should have four or five assumptions.

Because an assumption is a guess, it is also a risk. It should be considered in terms of its likelihood and effect, but it may be determined that the project can endure the risk. For example, it may be assumed that everyone on the project will work an eight-hour day until the job is completed. The project will, therefore, live with the risk that some people may work fewer hours or be called to work on other projects.

You should make allowance for the unforeseen, and include elements of tolerance and contingency. These are usually expressed as a flat percentage. Tolerance is the amount of time you can slip in the plan without reporting it to senior staff and seeking permission to continue. Contingency is an estimated amount of money, calculated when a project is being planned, to address identified risks and changes that the project may encounter. Tolerance and contingency are related to risk. The greater the risk, the more likely the project is to take longer and cost more. Tolerance of around 10% and contingency of 15% are usually suitable for a medium-scale project taking six months or less.

CHAPTER 3

Leading and Managing Teams

A leader takes people where they want to go. A great leader takes people where they don't necessarily want to go, but ought to be.

Rosalynn Carter

Never tell people how to do things. Tell them what to do and they will surprise you with their ingenuity.

George Patton

To handle yourself, use your head; to handle others, use your heart.

Eleanor Roosevelt

3.1 BECOMING THE PROJECT MANAGER

Project managers oversee activities, serve as the liaison between participating organizations, and facilitate project meetings. They hire staff, represent the project at meetings, prepare reports, attend professional development and project activities, and review project instructional materials. Project managers fulfill several human-resources-type responsibilities during a project. These functions include negotiating with resource managers, assigning tasks, developing job descriptions, identifying training needs, creating a project organization chart, producing a team roster, and developing a staffing management plan.

In essence, project managers assume responsibility for the achievement of project goals and objectives. Becoming a successful project manager requires a number of characteristics (Table 3.1) and skills (Table 3.2). Project managers also perform many duties (Table 3.3).

One of the biggest problems is how to be a working project manager—one who handles performing work in addition to managing the project. For small teams of up to four people, a project manager can do some of the work. As team size increases, it becomes impossible to work and manage simultaneously because the tasks will distract you from the needs of team members. When a conflict between managing and working exists, performing tasks takes priority and management is neglected. Often, working project managers choose the best tasks for themselves. This gives them a feeling of accomplishment, since it is easier to tell when you are done with

Project Management for Information Professionals
ISBN 978-0-08-100127-1

Table 3.1 Project Manager Characteristics

- Open-mindedness
- Trustworthiness
- Understanding
- Accountability
- Honesty and authenticity
- Emotional intelligence
- Calmness in the face of adversity
- Ability to inspire and elicit the best in others
- Self-confidence
- Problem solving
- Initiative
- Enthusiasm
- Adaptability
- Flexibility
- Positive outlook
- Self-awareness
- High tolerance for ambiguity and uncertainty
- Persuasiveness
- Ability to think like a generalist
- Assertiveness
- Political and cultural awareness

Table 3.2 Project Manager Skills

- Planning
- Problem solving
- Goal setting
- Negotiation
- Communications
- Interviewing
- Group dynamics
- Quality management
- Time management
- Decision making
- Conflict management
- Data analysis
- Leadership
- Written communication
- Coaching and counseling
- Team building
- Listening
- Scheduling methods
- Earned value analysis
- Organization
- Change management
- Delegation
- Technical knowledge

Table 3.3 Project Manager Duties

- Define the project
- Prepare the project plan
- Present the project and project plan
- Convey the purpose of the project
- Implement policies and procedures
- Apply effective project management methods and tools
- Interact with senior executives
- Interact with functional managers
- Obtain and coordinate the use of project resources
- Cooperate with users and vendors
- Interact with other projects
- Prepare, review, and revise budgets
- Review milestones
- Develop and revise schedules
- Manage the team
- Delegate responsibilities
- Define issues, problems, and opportunities
- Participate in specific project tasks
- Analyze issues
- Prepare and make presentations
- Determine project statuses
- Deal with conflict with management and within the project team
- Restructure the project plan
- Understand the tools and methods used in the project
- Learn from previous projects
- Deal with the impacts of project change
- Coordinate the addition and removal of team members

a task then when you are finished with a management initiative. The fallacy of this approach is twofold. First, a detailed assignment might take time away from project management responsibilities. Secondly, by taking the interesting jobs for themselves, working project managers deprive others of meaningful work, decrease their motivation, and send signals that they mistrust their teams.

The role of the project manager is to monitor performance and identify variances in the project plan, then take corrective action. The execution of the work itself is not a project management role, even if, as so often happens with small projects, the project manager is also doing some or most of the work. The project manager should focus on controlling the project, not on performing the work.

If organizations do not fully understand what project management is about, they may expect that it is feasible for individuals to do both. As a result, nearly everyone in the organization tries to manage projects. Some of them will be excellent at it, and others will be inept. A better approach is to select a few individuals who have the desire to be project managers and allow them to manage some projects. The other people are then free to do technical work without worrying about administrative issues, thus allowing project managers to excel at their jobs.

At some time during a project something will go wrong, or a change will be requested that may risk the project missing its time and cost targets. For this reason, organizations should give project managers the authority within specific parameters to carry out their jobs without having to seek approval for changes to costs or deadlines. Agreeing to manage by exception removes the confusion of who is authorized to take charge when problems or changes arise.

General management functions are related to the functions of the project manager and, in many cases, overlap with his or her responsibilities. It is important for the project manager to understand the connection between his or her role as an integrator for planning and management of the project team. To be successful, project managers must be aware of the organizational environment, which includes cultural, social, international, political, and physical aspects.

Project execution requires the traditional skills of management: keeping people motivated and focused on goals, mediating between layers of organizational hierarchy, making decisions, and allocating scarce resources to their best uses. The project manager must also control adherence to the schedule, budget, and quality standards. He or she must give particular attention to the kinds of issues concerning team-based work: interpersonal conflict, collaboration, and communication.

The most successful manager will be able to choose and use techniques that best suit the project. There is more to managing a project of any significant size than the application of a few procedures. It involves a whole framework of progressive planning and decisions, perceptiveness, common sense, organization, financial management, documentation, and a grasp of proven, long-established principles of management and leadership.

Most project managers will become accustomed to dealing with information that is incomplete, optimistic, inaccurate, or misleading. Above all else, they should be savvy. They check the information they receive by knowing what questions to ask to prove validity. As they gain experience in a particular organization, they become capable of assessing people's reliability so that they can apply confidence factors to the information supplied to them.

Project managers use the traditional project tools and techniques to reveal relevant project data. They understand that the tools are useless without clear thinking to ensure that the data is relevant and meaningful to the project. They arm their teams with a rational approach to managing aspects of a project, from defining the needs to constructing the plan to implementation. In the end, project success hinges on the quality of thinking behind the project management tools.

Project managers should be adept at steering the performance of their contributors while negotiating for resources and communicating status and priorities to upper management. They pay strict attention to project needs to resolve issues efficiently: making decisions, solving problems, and promoting opportunities.

With this in mind, a reasonable criterion can be identified for the selection of the project manager. A project manager is granted the authority to manage across several organizational lines. His or her activities resemble many aspects of general management, and must be performed well to continue to receive managerial support. Project management will not succeed without effective project managers. Thus if executive management approves a project for implementation, it should ensure that a qualified, reliable person is selected as the project manager. A project manager is much more likely to gain the support of the team and functional managers to accomplish desired goals if it is apparent that the organization's executive management has selected the project manager.

The project manager is focused on getting things accomplished, which requires the ability to work through influences within the organization. Executives must be kept involved in the decision-making process so that they do not interfere with the project manager's authority to press the project forward.

Not everyone makes a good project manager. The better ones tend to be well organized and willing to do whatever it takes to keep their projects on time and on budget. Charisma is the difference between competent and exceptional project managers. Sometimes it takes some charm to motivate people to deliver their best work under challenging circumstances.

The project manager also interacts with the rest of the organization on behalf of the team. He or she should be politically aware, and possess excellent negotiation skills to commit stakeholders who are initially resistant to the project. In addition the project manager must maintain resilience, as problems and setbacks arise throughout the project.

3.2 DEVELOPING LEADERSHIP SKILLS

A project manager's authority differs depending on the organization's structure. The structures that offer the highest to the least amount of power are in the following order: projectized, strong matrix, balanced matrix, weak matrix, and functional (Table 3.4).

The functional organization is a traditional company with well-defined divisions. Each department has a structured chain of authority that indicates who is in charge of each group and has the power to make decisions. Authority runs vertically, with gateways between divisions. It would be

Table 3.4 Organizational Types

Organizational Type	Pros	Cons
Projectized	The project manager controls the project decisions. The team focuses on project work without distractions.	Project teams may compete for or stockpile resources. Team members may lose focus near the end of the project because they are uncertain about their next assignment.
Strong matrix	The project manager has a high level of authority. Team members are assigned to 50—90% of the project's duration.	Competition over resources still exists. Costs may be high due to redundant administrative staff among projects.
Balanced matrix	The project manager shares authority with senior executives.	The project manager and functional manager may fight for team members' time. Team members may feel they are reporting to multiple bosses.
Weak matrix	The project manager acts as a coordinator with little authority.	The project is part of the functional department operations rather than a separate activity. People may be divided among many projects simultaneously.
Functional	Ideal for organizations with recurring projects. The functional manager is in charge.	The project manager has little authority and acts as a project expeditor.

unusual to find a conflict about who has authority over a particular area. The functional organization is similar to a group of silos; at times, it is difficult to communicate between them. As a result, change is challenging.

At the other end of the spectrum is the projectized organization. In this type of organization, projects are a significant portion of the work. As a result, structures are in place to promote project work. Many employees do not have a permanent assignment beyond their current project team. Instead of the vertical structure of a functional organization, there is a more flexible structure that changes as projects begin, continue, and close.

Often there are support personnel who handle project team members' needs, such as human resources, but the team members' manager is the project manager. Teams are made up of people who have expertise in the diverse areas that are required by the project. They are supported by centers of expertise, one of which would be project management.

In the projectized organization, the project manager has significant authority over not only team members but also the projects. Achieving a projectized organization is difficult, which is why more functional and matrix organizations exist.

Matrix organizations combine the characteristics of both functional and projectized organizations to varying degrees. Most archives, libraries, and museums fall into this category. Over time, many memory institutions have evolved from a functional to a matrix structure, through the flattening of the organization, the removal of management levels, and the formation of working groups (Bloss, 1997).

There are many advantages and disadvantages of matrix organizations (Table 3.5). Three classifications subsist within the domain of matrix organizations: strong, balanced, and weak. Each denotes organizations that have various functional and projectized organization characteristics.

The strong matrix organization resembles the projectized organization. Many employees are involved in project work. Rather than being assigned to a project team permanently, many employees reside in functional areas and are lent to projects. Few, if any, obligations from their functional areas occur during a project. For the most part, team members are focused on one or more projects at any given time.

Like the projectized organization, part of the role of the functional areas is to support project work. The most important aspect of the strong matrix organization is the function of project management. Project managers usually belong in a separate area in the organization and are assigned to projects. It is also important to note that the project manager has significant

Table 3.5 Advantages and Disadvantages of Matrix Organizations

Advantages	Disadvantages
Suitable for project-oriented organizations	Good people will be in demand for projects; others will sit in the unassigned pool
Ensures that people are used on projects	Difficult to balance control between project and functional management
Project manager tends to be successful in getting resources	Functional managers tend to be weak
Useful methods for accountability and tracking of projects	Lengthy projects seem like functional activities
Likelihood that people build skills through multiple projects	Hard to share resources between projects
Provides structure for medium to large projects	Hard for lessons and skills to cross projects
Ability to track the project work	Difficult to anticipate needs and staff

authority in a strong matrix organization, although not as much as in a projectized organization.

The balanced matrix organization takes its characteristics equally from projectized and functional organizations. Employees, including project managers, come from different functions within the organization. Usually project management is not a separate function, but expertise that is developed within a functional area. The project manager has less authority in this organization, but enough power to run a team effectively.

The weak matrix organization is similar to the functional organization. Team members come from different functional areas, and often continue working in their fields along with the project. A project coordinator without significant authority manages the team. One of the biggest challenges to this structure is getting team members to do project work. They often see projects as a burden rather than as part of their jobs. Because many weak matrix organizations still have a vertical structure, their managers may not be sympathetic to project needs. Strong leadership from the sponsor is required for a project to succeed.

As a project manager, you are expected to be both a good manager and a leader to be effective. An ability to lead is one of the most critical competencies a project manager must have. Project managers should be knowledgeable in all areas of authority for continuing success. Superficially charismatic managers, for example, may have initial appeal, but as problems arise that they are not able to assist, their power will be undermined. The project manager's leadership ability is usually expressed in terms of influencing the behavior and attitudes of the project team. The effectiveness of a leader is therefore dependent to some extent on his or her power.

Projects are often undertaken in environments where the project manager has little formal authority. Even for project managers who do have authority, contributors who work for other managers do portions of project work. Projects with no one in charge are almost certain to fail. As a leader of your project, you must assume control whether you possess the authority or not.

Leadership is both a property and a process (Griffin, 2008). Essentially, leadership can be seen as a combination of who a person is (property) and what that person does (process). Some people do not have the obvious characteristics of a leader, but their actions are what inspires others, whereas other leaders may not always seem to act accordingly, but who they are can be enough to motivate followers.

Leadership qualities include drive, the ability to take risks, experience with the type of project at hand, and a sense of the big picture. The differences between managers and leaders are displayed in their attributes (Table 3.6) and skills (Table 3.7).

Table 3.6 Manager and Leader Attributes

Attributes	Managers	Leaders
Team relationship	Have direct reports	Have followers
Role	Have team work for them	Work for the team
Style	Administer work	Direct people
Decision	Make decisions	Facilitate decisions
Directs	Dictate how and when	Persuade what and why
Power	Use authority	Use influence
Energy	Are controlling	Are passionate
Wants	Desire results	Desire achievement
Concern	Want to be right	Want to do what is right
Credit	Take	Give
Blame	Give	Take

Table 3.7 Management and Leadership Skill Differences

Management Skills	Leadership Skills
Define individual roles and responsibilities and assign the organizational structure	Set the vision for the project and its strategy
Mobilize the team	Create a shared vision with the team
Induct members into the team	Position the project in a wider context
Assign tasks to team members and set goals	Define and role-model the style of behavior wanted from the team
Provide levels of support based on allocated tasks	Motivate the project team
Set priorities	Adapt behavior for the situation
Provide learning opportunities for team members	Create an environment that encourages the best in team members
Define the management process for the project team	Influence stakeholders to facilitate delivery of the project
Motivate the team	Encourage team members to develop and learn
Resolve team and project conflicts and issues	Listen, counsel, and mentor team members
Provide performance feedback and guidance	Adapt the style to the situation
Appraise, manage, and reward the team	
Ensure quality of deliverables	
Provide project management expertise and put controls and management processes in place	

As a leader, it is important to view people as allies, not adversaries, and focus on common goals. Bolton (2005) notes, "The emphasis of the future has to be in the leadership and interpersonal skills that ensure sound project-management practices. Projects fail because relationships and expectations fail" (p. 64). Making people feel comfortable and valued encourages

Table 3.8 Influence Types

Type	Description
Legitimate	Authority based on a position within an organization
Coercive	Control based on intimidation
Reward	Influence based on the capacity to supply or withhold incentives
Expert	Clout based on a person's expertise or knowledge
Referent	Power that is transferred from an executive to a project manager

brainstorming, creative thinking, and a willingness to try new ideas, all of which are essential to managing a successful project. Cervone (2005) asserts:

> Many people think technology is the issue, but [project] complexity is more typically in the relationships between the various people involved in the project. You can be a more effective project manager by continuously using and developing behaviors that enhance your ability to influence others (p. 109).

Project managers can use various influence types to get desired results (Table 3.8). Apply this knowledge of different sources of power to increase your influence as a project manager.

Project managers must be committed to leading their teams to success. Frequently they must work without high-level support, at times with active resistance, and occasionally in the absence of evidence that the project is possible. Courageous leadership in the face of obstacles is required.

3.3 WORKING WITH STAKEHOLDERS

People are fundamental to every aspect of a project. They commission projects, provide resources, support or challenge projects, and contribute their energy to produce projects. People deliver projects as leaders, managers, and team members, and others influence projects as sponsors, stakeholders, and advisors. With so many people involved, projects are influenced by how people behave and feel about the project.

A stakeholder has an interest in a project's outcome. The project manager must consider the stakeholders' attitude toward the project, their influence on the organization, and their authority levels. Understanding a stakeholder's stance on the situation can help the project manager gather requirements and manage the stakeholder more effectively. A stakeholder interview template may be found in Appendix E.

Users are stakeholders. They are often called customers, end users, clients, or recipients of the project deliverables. These stakeholders can be library patrons, archives users, or museum visitors.

As one type of stakeholder, functional managers are not necessarily affiliated with a project team, nor are they directly involved in the day-to-day management of the project. Functional managers are resource providers for the team and can significantly affect a project's success.

Another type of stakeholder is a subject-matter expert. These experts are authorities possessing specialized knowledge on certain aspects of the project. Subject-matter experts provide advice to projects on an as-needed basis. They ensure that the teams they work with gain the information and insight needed to get the job done. Subject-matter experts tend to possess cross-departmental expertise. They are often considered indispensable operationally and, for this reason, are not assigned full-time project team memberships. It is common for subject-matter experts to span multiple projects concurrently, allowing them to share knowledge across a multitude of efforts.

Another stakeholder is the business analyst. He or she identifies the business needs of the organization and helps determine solutions to problems. The business analyst completes requirements development and performs requirement management. He or she also facilitates communications among users, stakeholders, and the team members.

The relationships between stakeholder roles are functional rather than hierarchical. Although the sponsor will usually be the most senior member of the project team and will be higher ranking than the manager, little else can be assumed about the seniority of other team members. Subject-matter experts and technical specialists, in particular, frequently have skills based on years of experience and are often senior to the project manager.

For large, complex projects like the building or renovation of libraries, archives, or museums, several project teams are formed to move the process forward. Representatives from the governing authority, the board of trustees, the administration and staff, friends' groups, and community interest groups may be part of this collective. Usually a smaller working group is formed from the larger group of stakeholders to expedite the process, and its decisions are brought back to the larger group for review and approval. Whatever team is formed, it is vital that only one person—usually the project manager—speaks for the entire organization in dealing with consultants and contractors during the design and building process.

To identify stakeholders, pay attention to the individuals who will be affected by your project's outcomes: the contributors of resources, including people, space, time, tools, and money, and the beneficiaries of the project's output. Each is a stakeholder in your project.

Stakeholders influence a project throughout its life cycle and contribute to its success (Table 3.9). During planning they assist in defining objectives, requirements, and constraints; identify strategies; evaluate the plan and

Table 3.9 Stakeholders and their Contributions

Stakeholders	Contributions
Application architect	Defines the technical direction for the project, creates the architectural approach, and serves as project expert for the structure of the project.
Business analyst	Elicits, documents, and reviews project requirements.
Database analyst	Designs, creates, and maintains databases for the project.
Developer	Serves as a technical resource on the project; may serve as a designer, tester, coder, and application developer.
Functional managers	Establish company policies; provide people for the team.
Information architect	Helps assess the project's data requirements, identifies data assets, and helps the team complete data modeling requirements.
Infrastructure analyst	Designs the software, hardware, and technical infrastructure for the project.
Operational managers	Manage the core business areas of the organization.
Program managers	Responsible for related projects.
Project team	Provides skills, expertise, and exertion to perform the work.
Quality assurance analyst	Ensures that the deliverables meet the quality requirements and manages quality standards compliance.
Sponsor	Provides authority and financial resources; guides the selection process and helps develop the initial scope and charter.
Users	Those who will use the product created by the project. Establishes the requirements for the project; reviews the project as milestones and deliverables are met. Accepts the finished product.
Vendors	External companies that supply equipment or services necessary for the project.

schedule; and provide funding. During implementation stakeholders do the work, resolve issues, decide whether changes are necessary, and control the budget. Although the users and the sponsor are the most important people to please, a project is successful if it pleases most, if not all, stakeholders.

Stakeholders can make or break a project. Some people may have concerns but no power to change anything in the project. Others may be supportive but lack rank. The opposite is also true: some important individuals may be the champions or nay-sayers for your project. You need to know who you can trust for support, but you also want to know who may cause you to lose traction. Hackman (1990) advises regarding projects that inaugurate archives:

> Ordinarily no one actor [or stakeholder] has exclusive or enduring influence, but that in most settings, influential actors arrive and depart relatively frequently. The archival program developer need not be paralyzed by the past views or policies of the people in positions of authority; in fact, there are seemingly quite a few opportunities to influence those views or otherwise to change present policy. It seems especially useful to act when the situation is fluid as it usually is when a new player arrives… Even a broad new institution-wide initiative… can be seized upon if it has been broadly accepted or is identified with an especially influential resource allocator (p. 551).

In the course of a project, key individuals who are supporters or antagonists may change, and understanding their attitudes and interests is important in continuing a project smoothly.

The project manager should create a strategy that satisfies those with high power within the organization. A stakeholder matrix plots the power and interest levels of your stakeholders (Figure 3.1). On the vertical axis, power is determined to be low, medium, or high; on the horizontal axis, interest in the project is gauged as low, medium, or high.

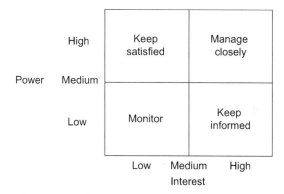

Figure 3.1 Stakeholder Power and Influence Matrix

Stakeholders in the low/low quadrant should be monitored. You should communicate with them as needed according to your communication management plan. Stakeholders in the low power/high interest portion of the grid should be kept informed. They need to know about progress and changes, but do not merit further involvement. Stakeholders landing in the high power/low interest quadrant should be kept satisfied. Be diligent with this group; involve them as needed to help you achieve project success. The stakeholders that are evaluated as having high power and high interest should be managed closely, because they may be members of your steering committee or change control board. Ascertain and respond to any questions or concerns they have in a timely fashion.

Project sponsors are senior executives responsible for shepherding projects to a successful conclusion. For project management to be successful within an organization, it must have executive support. The sponsor must champion the benefits of the project, accept responsibility for funding and budget statuses, concur with project and charter requirements, and be knowledgeable about planned and actual results. Sponsors have the duty to assist their project teams in resolving organizational impediments to project success. They work with project managers to ensure a smooth transition from project inception to completion. In fact, the aim of experienced project managers is to ensure executive involvement throughout their projects' life cycle by forging solid relationships with their projects' sponsors. There is little a project manager will not share with her or his project sponsor. In turn, by addressing challenging project issues and concerns as they arise, sponsors hedge risk and improve outcomes.

When establishing a relationship with the sponsor, the project manager should become familiar with organizational policies, procedures, standards, and culture. Knowledge of these matters may assist in defining expectations and developing strategies for managing issues that may require sponsor involvement. There are also other ways to forge a good relationship with the sponsor (Table 3.10).

Leifer et al. (2000) made an important observation about each of the 10 projects they studied. They discovered that a highly placed sponsor was instrumental in providing critical services. The sponsors kept their projects active by providing funding, through normal channels and other means. They deflected attempts to terminate innovative projects and promoted the value of project goals to higher management. Without the support of these patrons, the projects would have been futile.

Table 3.10 Tips for a Good Sponsor-Manager Relationship

- Inspire confidence that you are the right person for the project.
- Establish personal rapport with the sponsor.
- Ask about the other projects he or she has sponsored to determine his or her work style.
- Agree upon how you should interact when things go wrong.
- Find out from the sponsor what information he or she requires, its frequency, and format.

When writing about instituting an archives program at the Archdiocese of Boston, O'Toole (1990) advises, "The support from the top was essential, though the archives recognized the fragility of relying too much on the interest of specific individuals, no matter how highly placed or well disposed" (p. 552). The sponsor is important, but it is also useful to maintain the support of as many senior executives as possible.

Some stakeholders will exert enormous influence on the project, like sponsors who provide political, financial, and logistical support, champion the project, and approve its results. If you are working on a project that is your idea and you have the means to accomplish it without drawing on additional resources, you may feel the project does not need a sponsor. However, it is worth considering whether you could ask someone to act in that capacity so that you have a sounding board for the project. Even if every aspect of the project falls within your areas of responsibility, you are committing the organization's resources if you are spending your time on the project. Gaining the support of a senior manager to act as the sponsor will ensure that you have the approval of your organization to perform the project. It might also be more beneficial to the organization if your project helps others to consider alternative ways of achieving objectives, and you may find that your idea becomes a pilot project for wider use.

3.4 DEVELOPING THE TEAM

The most advantageous size for a project team depends on the project's goals and tasks. The ideal team size depends on its application. Teams tend to grow until they get large enough to subdivide into cliques. A project manager should strive to have just enough people to do the job. Having too few people slows down work and members may lack requisite skills. Having too many will also impede progress by shifting time and energy to communication and coordination efforts. Commitment may also be a

Table 3.11 Project Team Candidate Questions

- Do they have suitable knowledge and skills, including technical, functional, or problem solving?
- Do they have the desired personal characteristics for the project?
- Do they believe in project's goals and seem likely to support it?
- Do they have the time to devote to the project?
- Are they compatible with other team members under consideration?
- Do they regard project participation as welcome or as an intrusion on their regular responsibilities?

problem, as individual dedication to the team and its goals diminishes as more people are added. Recruit as many people as you need to get the job done. The experts suggest between five and 10 people. Katzenbach and Smith (1993) offer cues to know whether your team is the right size: the team convenes and communicates easily, and no additional people are required to get the job done.

The appropriate team size depends on how many people are needed to perform the work for the project, the project's complexity, and if the project requires a variety of technical expertise. If the team is too small, it may not have the knowledge and skills to meet the needs of the project. The odds of conflict increase with the number of people in the team. Large teams tend to be unwieldy, unable to reach agreement or collect everyone's contribution, and may find communication and cooperation difficult. The team also needs a balance of personalities. Some questions can be used to determine suitable candidates for the project (Table 3.11).

Project teams do not have the luxury of a couple of months of adjustment. In a project environment, teams are expected to start reaching milestones and delivering tasks after the kick-off meeting. Sponsors think that teams will automatically gel, but experienced project managers know that this is rarely the case.

Those who are on the initiation team work together to confirm that there is a project to do. This group may not be the team that works to deliver the project, but the project manager can still use team management skills to keep the discussions on track and build consensus. Once the team is determined, make a project roster. A template can be found in Appendix E.

Team management activities during the initiation phase are setting roles and responsibilities, even if some of the team members who will fulfill those roles are unassigned. Search for team members whom you would want to join the project, bearing in mind how the individuals would work together.

Start thinking about the environment you wish to create: what will be the project's values, culture, and rules? This may change as you bring others on to the team in later phases, but it is a good idea to spend time thinking about this now.

As the project progresses, the team rallies and the real effort of team-building starts. Up to this point, the principal relationships have been between the project manager and each team member, which puts much responsibility on the project manager. You probably know the individuals better than they know each other, so the team members will come to you for help and guidance instead of going to each other. You have two responsibilities: getting to know the individuals better yourself, and facilitating them in getting to know each other. The project manager and team members share responsibilities to make the project successful (Table 3.12).

The project manager must focus energy and attention on building the team. A well-managed and motivated team is more likely to commit to the project objectives than a loosely formed group. Techniques for teambuilding include management abilities, interpersonal skills, training, activities, co-location, and recognition. Highly functional teams share many characteristics (Table 3.13).

Developing a team that crosses many departments may be advantageous as well. In writing about American University developing a campus-wide image database, Albrecht (2007) states:

> If you are working with a group of colleagues who represent a good cross-section of the campus community, your project will get more notice, will enjoy greater support, and will have the potential to expand in different ways... Collaboration efforts can open up general support and funding opportunities and thus allow the project to expand beyond the scope of the individual unit (p. 52).

Working with the IT team, the College of Arts and Sciences, and the university library brought more technical assistance, funding, and institutional support, as well as recognition of the project among the community.

When you are building a team, ensure that everyone feels included—otherwise your efforts may backfire, and the team will fall apart. Teambuilding activities, when not managed effectively, can trigger issues for people regarding rejection and social hierarchy.

Teambuilding occurs as people work together on a project. Over time, team members form alliances and make friends. However, even the most

Table 3.12 Project Manager and Team Member Responsibilities

Project Manager Responsibilities	Team Member Responsibilities
Organize, monitor, and control project	Attend meetings
Stimulate group interaction	Commit to the project
Promote participative planning	Provide accurate and truthful status updates
Manage conflict in a constructive manner	Take direction, but push back appropriately
Keep the costs, meetings, and administration to a minimum	Agree to realistic targets and deadlines
Ensure that information about the project is communicated to the stakeholders	Complete project tasks
Keep the team informed of all developments	Inform team of current or potential problems
Give feedback and to support the team	Suggest solutions to problems
Keep the project aligned with the organization's policies and procedures	Support team members and the project manager
Ensure that the project complies with legal requirements	Manage their own time for project and routine activities
Advise based on their roles as generalists	Advise based on their roles as subject-matter experts
Focus on project and overall goals	Focus on individual goals
Resist unnecessary changes	Maintain a positive attitude
Recognize and reward achievement	Be respectful of other team members

extroverted people experience anxiety early in the process as they wonder how well the team will work together. You can use teambuilding activities to help alleviate this initial reticence by sharing experiences, expectations, and goals.

There is a commitment to the team and to the individuals on the team. Many teams have shortcuts and a shared vocabulary. Team members are also interested in how their teammates are doing. If one teammate seems overworked or stressed, another team member may relieve his or her workload.

Psychologist Bruce Tuckman (1938-) theorized that teams have to go through five stages of group development before they truly become a

Table 3.13 Highly Functional Team Characteristics

- Meet stakeholder expectations
- Improve processes
- Embrace change
- Create and use ground rules
- Have mutual accountability
- Employ creativity
- Formulate joint decisions
- Take initiative
- Contribute their highest level of experience and expertise
- Demonstrate good faith and goodwill, focusing on what is best for the team
- Subordinate personal agendas to the will of the majority
- Honor individual diversity and contributions
- Demonstrate respectful communication and confidentiality
- Express trustworthiness while extending trust to others
- Relinquish the need to control all decisions
- Practice good listening skills

team: forming, storming, norming, performing, and adjourning (1965). Lipnack and Stamps (2000) later added a testing phase.

Forming is the trial balloon phase. Someone has an idea, and starts building interest, sponsorship, and alliances. During this phase many discussions occur, serving to build support and consensus about the vision. The project manager creates a team. Everyone gets to know each other and ensures that the infrastructure and executive support are in place so that the project can succeed. Managers can harness this initial burst of productivity by setting appropriate expectations, ensuring a path free of obstacles, and directing activities.

The storming stage displays the differences among team members about vision, expectations, work methods, and communication styles. During this phase guidelines are honed, compromises are made, and bonding takes place. Managers help shorten this period of conflict by facilitating discussions, documenting decisions, modeling behaviors, reducing power struggles, and redirecting people to the larger purpose of the project.

During the norming stage teambuilding begins in earnest, as individuals become comfortable with each other and with their roles. The team identifies activities or solutions that are easy to implement and have a positive impact on the direction and pace of the project. Managers can assist the team by providing opportunities for social interaction and encouraging open discussions and creative problem solving, as well as identifying the go-to people for specific activities.

During the performing stage the team works well together and independently. Managers can maximize the benefit of this stage by removing roadblocks, verifying that the team has all the tools it needs to accomplish the tasks, establishing criteria, and delegating tasks.

Testing is the verification phase. As parts of the project are completed, they are confirmed against the specifications and other components of the project. The team identifies and corrects problems. Managers can facilitate the testing phase by ensuring that the tools and processes are working correctly and open communication exists between developers and the testers. Often this is a period of stress as assumptions and previous work are tested against performance expectations.

In the adjourning phase the team finishes its tasks, evaluates activities, and prepares to transition to other projects. Conflict occurs during this stage because of the stress of deadlines and the uncertainty associated with change. Managers can ease the transition by making sure that team and individual efforts are recognized, offering an opportunity to discuss the project, and providing direction on what team members should focus on next.

There are several team development theories. American psychologist Abraham Maslow (1908–1970) created a hierarchy of needs (1943): a theory of psychological health predicated on fulfilling innate human needs. Physiological needs include those required for sustaining human life, such as food, water, warmth, and shelter. Maslow believed that until these physiological needs have been met, other motivational factors have little impact. Safety is the necessity to feel free from threat, danger, or physical or emotional harm. Social needs are the need for company, affection, and interaction. Esteem concerns our desires for recognition, being held in high regard by others, and feelings of accomplishment. Self-actualization is the highest level of human need and concerns our drive to achieve our full potential. Maslow suggested that it is also associated with altruistic behavior.

In his hygiene theory (1968), American psychologist Frederick Herzberg (1923–2000) postulated a theory in which he identified hygiene factors that make employees dissatisfied and motivation factors that provide a positive impetus. Hygiene agents are the expectations that workers have regarding job security, a paycheck, safe working conditions, a sense of belonging, good working relationships, and other employment basics. Motivating agents include responsibility, appreciation of work, recognition, education, and other opportunities beyond financial rewards. He suggested that intrinsic factors are related to motivators because extrinsic factors are associated with dissatisfaction. Whereas Maslow was not concerned solely with the working environment, Herzberg's model is explicitly so defined. Removal of job security, reasonable pay, good supervisors, or ·pleasant working conditions causes dissatisfaction. Reinforcement of an employee's sense of worth, value, praise, and achievement drive positive motivation. For people to excel, motivating factors must exist.

Douglas McGregor (1906–1964) at the MIT Sloan School of Management developed the Theory X and Theory Y theories of human motivation (1960). McGregor suggested that people in organizations could be managed in one of two ways depending on their attitude to work. Theory X people are employed because they have to work, and will do as little as possible or avoid work all together. They need a carrot-and-stick management style and resist taking on new responsibilities. Usually they are more concerned with security needs than with esteem needs such as achievement and ambition. Theory Y people find work stimulating and energizing; they want to be a part of a successful organization. They are imaginative and creative, and seek new responsibilities and challenges to stretch their capabilities. They are actively engaged employees who will bring discretionary effort and expertise into their work.

Keeping in mind these various motivation factors and theories will assist you as a project manager to get the best out of your team. Being able to encourage others to perform project work is an essential factor in successful projects.

3.5 DETERMINING ROLES

Project work enables people to undertake roles that differ from their usual work. Projects provide a training ground for teamwork and leadership. Most project team members will probably be part of your core team and focused primarily on your project, but your team may also include others who are as yet unidentified. Team members may have other responsibilities in addition to your project, and these contributors may pose problems for a project manager with limited authority. Identify any skill gaps or resource shortfalls, and then begin to work to locate people to resolve staffing issues.

People should be included in a project only as long as they have tasks to perform. Always observe the principle that the right to make decisions on professionally related questions belongs to those who have daily responsibility for them. Consult the right people.

Knowing how to bring together a group of people and create a high-performing team is an essential skill for a project manager. However, team management activities depend on where you are in the project management life cycle. Although you are managing a team from day one, how you go about doing that is different from what you will end up doing halfway through the project or at its end. The evolution of skills will determine how to establish roles within the team to maximize its efficiency and identify opportunities to cultivate the capabilities of project team members.

As teams work together, informal roles develop. One person may enjoy planning meetings while another might have an aptitude for troubleshooting. Project managers take advantage of these diverse skills by delegating tasks to the people who enjoy doing them and are good at them. Doing so enriches everyone's experiences and builds ownership into the project.

Project teams are a way of managing projects where efficiency performs the work well; effectiveness acts upon the right work. The team should share the volume of work, which can be resolved while determining roles for team members. The project's scope may require a range of skills that one person is unlikely to have. Brainstorming and discussions are good examples of interactive teamwork to generate ideas and solve problems. A small team can generate many options and alternatives; a suggestion from one person can stimulate ideas from others. The selected option should then have the support and commitment of the team, who will collectively share the risk of the decision. A team tends to make better decisions than its members would make individually with the same information. Exchanging ideas stimulates creativity and innovation.

Cross-functional teams, many of which are also geographically dispersed and multicultural, accomplish most of the work done by organizations today. What distinguishes an effective team from others? Technology is not enough. It is important to have shared team objectives, knowledge, equipment, abilities, and desire. Without these components in place, teams struggle. Without a shared vision and goals to support that vision, teams fracture along political or functional lines and the project fails.

Recruit people who already believe that the project's goals are important. They will be predisposed to concentrate on achieving these goals rather than thinking about the differences they have with other team members.

Engage members in activities they find interesting and worthy. This too will keep them focused on results. Publicly recognize the contributions of individual members to make them feel appreciated and part of the group. Acknowledge the value of diversity, and how team members serve the common goal. Unique skills and singular insights contribute to the success of the project.

Create opportunities for members to become friendly with each other. Whether it is through off-site recreation, shared lunches, or other activities, give people chances to get to know each other. Doing so will help them find a basis for collaborations.

A responsibility matrix, also known as an RACI matrix, presents the major activities in a project and the key stakeholder groups. It is a method to identify the roles within a project and the associated responsibilities for the project work. This matrix identifies the roles of the project participants, identifies their actions, and determines if you have all the roles to complete the responsibilities. Using the matrix can help avoid communication breakdowns between departments and organizations, because everyone involved can see who to contact for each activity. A template may be found in Appendix E.

The matrix uses a legend for each identified project task and each role in the project. Those marked "responsible" do the work and are accountable for its completion, quality, and adherence to defined requirements. Accountable members are the decision-makers regarding their tasks. People who are denoted "consult" must be conferred with before the work begins and serve as a point of information for the activity's resources. Team members who are indicated as "inform" need to be kept abreast of the activity's completion.

It is possible for more than one role to serve in multiple categories. For example, the metadata specialist could have both accountable and consult attributes on a particular activity. The accountable responsibility, however, should only be assigned to one role per activity. This is because you do not want multiple roles making decisions on each project assignment. For each task, assess whether the staffing seems adequate and whether you believe that the contributors involved are capable of the work. For each individual, check to see that he or she is not assigned more responsibility than seems appropriate.

3.6 EVALUATING PERFORMANCE

A problem for team members is that they become torn between the conflicting demands of their functional manager and their project

Table 3.14 Delegation Tips

- Set clear expectations.
- Explain assignments and provide needed resources.
- Make sure your team feels a sense of shared responsibility for the team's work.
- Recognize team member capabilities and interests.
- Trust your team's ability to get the job done.
- Focus on results, and resist the need to get involved in how tasks are undertaken.
- Regard delegation as a way to develop the skills of your team.
- Spread interesting tasks across the team.
- Delegate some tasks that increase team members' visibility within the organization.
- Assign work to the lowest possible level to make the best use of work resources.
- Provide coaching as needed.
- Deflect reverse delegation. Do not solve other's problems, but focus on generating alternatives together.
- Follow up to monitor progress.

manager. This situation arises if there is a lack of clarity in their work in their everyday duties and their project assignments. It can be a stressful situation. The best way of ensuring that it does not occur is for team members to start their work by clarifying the needs of the project and agreeing on boundaries. Additionally, delegation of work needs to be clear, and there are several tips for successful delegation (Table 3.14). Sometimes a three-way meeting with the team member, the project manager, and the functional manager can lead to an agreement and a set of boundaries for the project work.

Especially in matrixed organizations, do not assume that your tasks are the only tasks, or the highest-priority work, your team members are performing. Offer to work with each of them and their managers to ensure the workload being expected of them is reasonable. If necessary, try to rearrange task timing or sequencing, or assist your team members by having others help with their assignments.

Motivating team members on a project can be tricky. For the most part, project managers lack the authority to hire, fire, or reprimand team members; in most cases they do not even have the luxury of selecting them. However, they are still accountable for managing them to achieve the project objectives. Since they do not have much position power, they need to rely on motivation and influence.

There are interdependencies among team members. They depend on each other to get the job done. This includes an awareness of how one team member's work influences another member or the rest of the team. The team knows that every person is accountable for the team's success as a whole. Therefore, if a team member is not performing acceptably, another member may challenge his or her performance. In some cases individuals may need some help; in other instances their performance may be unacceptable. Either way, effective teams hold each other accountable in a respectful manner.

Team members trust each other. Each individual relies on other members to get the job done. If there are performance issues or differences in style, team members feel comfortable enough with each other to address variances in opinions, values, and attitudes. High-performing teams find ways to handle differences with methods that increase trust between members.

Teams demonstrate a high level of energy and achievement. They spend their time aimed at the target. They are clear about what the objectives and goals are, and they are focused on meeting them. Achievement fuels the energy and enthusiasm of the team. As members stay focused on achieving the goal together, their performance improves and their enthusiasm grows.

Focus on people's strengths rather than their weaknesses, and find a quality that you can respect in each person on your team. People enjoy their work more and work harder when others who appreciate their efforts surround them. When someone does something well, tell the person, the person's boss, and other team members that you appreciate the effort and its results. Recognizing good performance confirms the value of his or her work to the team member. Mention the quality of the results accomplished as well as the effort that he or she invested. Be specific: tell people exactly what they did or produced that you appreciate. Provide your feedback promptly; do not wait weeks or months before recognizing their work.

Try "management by walking around," a management style that involves wandering in an unstructured manner to check in with team members about the status of ongoing work. Be unpredictable and spontaneous. Practice and persistence will make it easier over time. Seek out your team members equally, not just the people who are easiest to find or with whom you are already friendly. Be approachable to everyone. You can also use the time for spontaneous recognition. If you see something good, compliment the team member. If you see activities that trouble you, talk to the team member in private at a later time.

3.7 TRACKING PROGRESS

Tracking is the process by which project progress is measured to ensure that changes to the schedule are promptly acted upon. Your starting point is the project baseline schedule and other plan documents devised and accepted before implementation, when key stages are fixed. The project baseline should remain unchanged throughout the project, and it is the guide against which variances are identified.

Team members need to know where their efforts fit into the larger project, how they are doing compared to other team members, and how the team fares compared to initial project estimates. Ensure that you have processes in place to allow team members to perform tasks. Team members should update progress on individual tasks. Project managers should view overall project status, adjust the plan as needed, maintain an archives for documenting actions and decisions, and calculate metrics that may help improve the accuracy of estimates for future projects.

While you must track progress, resist micromanaging your team. It lowers morale, fosters dependence, and discourages growth. Regardless of your intent, micromanaging tells your team members that you lack faith in their ability to do their work. The only times you may need to manage your team closely are when they are falling behind schedule or when a team member is not doing his or her job.

You should communicate with your team regularly. Do not wait to do this in project status meetings. Talk to individuals prior to meetings so that you are prepared to deliver the right message. If you ask on a continuous basis but are inconsistent in the elapsed time between checks, it conditions the team to move forward without your prodding.

Search for progress information from your team. If a task is supposed to begin, ask the team member if it did. If a task is finishing within a week, check its progress. Many project managers erroneously wait until a project status meeting to check how things are progressing. What some find is that nothing has occurred since the previous status meeting, and now an entire week has been lost.

Assume that your plan is set appropriately. The schedule will expand and contract based on early and late dates, and the project plan should be flexible to accommodate these variables. If tasks are finished early, continue the momentum by notifying team members to start the next task early. If a task is finishing late, you can talk with the team members to make sure they are ready to move on as soon as it finishes so that minimal time is lost.

When you begin tracking a project, ensure that you are keeping track of the information that will be most useful to you later. Track the cost of the project and the amount of effort expended, usually noted as hours devoted to each task or expenses accrued. Tracking the process involves a measurement of things that happened during the project, such as the number of review cycles. These metrics can include variance measurements, such as how far over or under budget you are or how far ahead or behind the estimated schedule. The output is the capacity of the finished project, such as the number of digitized images in a mass-digitization project. Be diligent in keeping current with the status of your plan. Record the actual hours expended and other measures appropriate to your project.

3.8 MANAGING EXPECTATIONS

Delivering a project on time, on budget, and with quality does not always mean you are successful. Your definition of the triple constraint may not be the same as the definition held by your sponsor or users. Even if their expectations of cost and speed are unrealistic, however, they are the final judges of your project. In their eyes the project may be late, over budget, or of poor quality.

It may seem unfair, but it does happen. This kind of disagreement, however, is preventable. Recognizing that the perceptions of others define a project's success is an incentive to make sure that all stakeholders agree on the basics. It is important to set realistic expectations with the project's stakeholders. Make sure you deliver the promised project, on time, and within budget.

To ensure that the stakeholders will believe a project is successful, you must manage expectations throughout the project. Managing expectations is crucial to success because it keeps expectations in line with the project's goals, objectives, and requirements. Otherwise, a stakeholder's definition of success will differ from yours. As a result, the project will be a failure in their eyes even if it follows the project management plan.

A communications plan (discussed in Chapter 6) and the previously discussed stakeholder matrix track the interests of those involved in your project and give the big picture about the expectations of stakeholders.

One of the most beneficial, yet neglected, activities in projects is clarifying mutual expectations with stakeholders (Table 3.15). Many people assume that they will know what the other parties are going to do, how they will behave, and what they will deliver. When expectations are

Table 3.15 Mutual Expectations

Users expect the project manager to:	The project manager expects users to:
• Understand their business needs • Understand their priorities (cost, time, scope) • Be capable of looking at the project from their perspective • Keep them informed of progress and changes	• Speak in terms of needs, not solutions • Articulate requirements in the process as early as possible • Provide information necessary to do the job • Minimize changes to the project

unclear, it results in rework, poor working relationships, misunderstandings, and dissatisfaction.

Discover what stakeholders expect by meeting with them individually. Since this is time-consuming, you may want to limit face-to-face meetings to key stakeholders. If there are differences between what they expect and what you believe they should anticipate, you should work out those differences as soon as possible.

Conversely, you can also express what you anticipate from stakeholders. However, some project managers have trouble expressing their expectations to members of management. If you feel this way, bear in mind that stating expectations does not mean you are telling them what to do or how to act. If you express yourself correctly, it should be a description of the support you need rather than a prescription for their behavior.

The project manager's assumptions and responses to questions and situations set the tone for the project. In addition, team members come to the project with assumptions and needs of their own. When establishing the team, it is important to identify such expectations and ensure that the team is focused on the same objectives and has the same expectations about the project.

Agree upon rules for communication between team members and with senior management, functional groups, users, and other employees. There should also be behavior expectations, especially regarding how to handle conflicts and disagreements within the team. Team members should agree on expectations for the percentage of available work time that each person will devote to the project, the relationship of the project to other priorities, and the hierarchy within the team.

Managing expectations within the team leads to better teambuilding. It is ideal to have the team determine its rules, as it best understands the individual needs of members. For example, they can agree on the start and stop times for workdays or when documents should be made available for review prior to meetings. The pursuit of a common approach includes how to debate and establish expectations for what each person brings to the working environment.

Establish your team's performance objectives as they relate to project requirements and expected benefits. These comprise the success criteria for assessing the outcomes of the project. Examples of these performance objectives include deadlines that have to be met and quality standards for the products of the project.

Teams with dispersed members present some challenges for a project manager. How will you know that they are working on what you want them to? How will you get in touch with them? Project managers also have a role in protecting the interests of the team at the home institution. Project managers with international responsibilities have to educate team members in how to work well together, and also have to manage upward and ensure that executive stakeholders understand the constraints of this type of project.

International projects take longer and entail higher travel costs than projects where the entire team is co-located, and that is not always a welcome message to senior management. Even small organizations can operate internationally by outsourcing to partners overseas, which means that project managers in these organizations face the challenges of managing multicultural teams.

For international projects, team members may have different rules and expectations about behavior. For example, the importance of being on time varies from culture to culture, as do many other aspects of work. Making these expectations explicit at the beginning helps to alleviate potential conflicts. Negotiating a team culture is important for ensuring mutual respect and understanding among team members.

While projects with an international element present particular challenges, teams that are based in the same country can find themselves working across different time zones. Even if you do not have this problem, you could still find it difficult to manage a project team split across several locations.

Part-time team members may have regular hours when they work on the project, for example every Monday and Wednesday. Alternatively, they might have particular tasks to do, and may work flexibly around these. A task may be programmed to last 16 hours, and they will split the hours across the week as required. This can make it difficult to schedule regular team meetings and one-on-one meetings with part-time team members. In the worst-case scenario, part-time members may not participate in meetings, saying that they are not scheduled to be working at that time. They may find that their other responsibilities limit their involvement.

Part-time team members are probably on loan from another manager, which creates a set of challenges. Your priorities will compete with the priorities of the functional manager, causing the team member to be in the middle of the conflict.

Even team members who work on your project on a full-time basis could have a different functional manager. While they might be yours for a period, team members in this situation are likely to have responsibilities in their original team. These are moments where you will have to negotiate with their functional managers to find the best possible solution to get the project work completed.

CHAPTER 4

Planning and Scheduling

Make no little plans; they have no magic to stir men's blood and probably themselves will not be realized. Make big plans; aim high in hope and work.

Daniel H. Burnham, American architect and urban designer

Plans are nothing; planning is everything.

Dwight D. Eisenhower

Chance favors the prepared.

Louis Pasteur

4.1 PREPARING THE PLAN

Planning is a dynamic process. Managing a project means keeping a balance between having a plan and responding to changes. Planning is iterative: the project team needs reevaluate the plan throughout the course of the project, and changes should be communicated to those involved to continue the project. Always prepare to replan, because obstacles will occur. The team should create an initial plan and begin to execute it, then do more planning and more executing. Momentum is generated by the accomplishment of incremental activities that the team said it would do. Progressive elaboration continuously improves the plan when more information becomes available as the project progresses.

The level of planning necessary for a project depends on the organizational culture and the nature of the project. Cervone (2009) notes that the planning process:

varies significantly from library to library. In some libraries, a well-developed and strictly followed process may be in place while in other libraries a more *laissez-faire* approach may be taken where the project just develops as things go along. In reality, neither approach is appropriate in every situation. Conditions will change and opportunities will arise that make it impossible or unwise to follow a rigid, formal process. On the other hand, a freewheeling approach to project development is highly unlikely to result in a good outcome (p. 16).

The most important aspect is to plan enough to improve your project outcome without becoming mired in too many details or levels of planning.

Project Management for Information Professionals
ISBN 978-0-08-100127-1

Table 4.1 Project Planning Benefits

- Communicating to others what you are going to do
- Reducing uncertainty
- Keeping up with rapid changes
- Avoiding limitations of intuitive reasoning
- Understanding the objectives
- Monitoring and controlling the work
- Providing goals
- Determining budgeting needs
- Providing needed time and schedule to achieve goals
- Gaining support from team members
- Ensuring that tasks are reviewed by team members

There are many benefits to creating a project plan (Table 4.1). A good plan explains the scope of the project in a way that the stakeholders and decision-makers agree upon and understand. It tells a story of how project work unfolds sequentially, and identifies the decision points and milestones that the project team must reach before additional work can proceed. It defines the roles and involvement of the project team. It presents a schedule of detailed activities and deliverables that show progress or lack thereof. It also introduces uncertainty in a manner that stakeholders can comprehend, so they can then take appropriate action.

For short, straightforward projects, the project plan can be a three- to five-page document. For larger, more complicated projects it may be 30–40 pages long. Regardless of length, the purpose of the plan is to document the proposed project in as much detail as possible before any work begins.

A mature project culture implies that everyone in the organization understands project management fundamentals. Projects should have plans at both global (or milestone) and detail (or activity) levels. Plans are controlled so everyone knows that variances are taken seriously. Once the plan is created, the project receives resources from the organization as agreed upon.

In organizations where there is an urgency to see results, the benefits of planning are often forgotten until it is too late. In many instances an organization does not produce plans because it is thought that there is not enough time to think ahead. For small projects, preparation is sometimes deemed unnecessary, and the risks associated with the absence of a plan are considered low enough not to warrant creating one. However, this does not recognize the likelihood of change. Change can affect even small projects or ones similar to those previously undertaken. The time used to develop a plan is used to understand how different the circumstances are since the last project was undertaken and how much more the situation may change during the life cycle of the next project.

A group should plan the project together. When you encourage your team members to participate in the planning process, you take the first step in developing your team as well as creating a more realistic plan. Woolridge et al. (2008) noted that involvement of staff in planning and strategic processes is a relatively recent concept:

> The recognition in the research literature of middle management's relevance to strategy formulation began in the 1970s. Up to that point, conceptualization of management generally, and strategy in particular, assumed a top-down analytical process that separated decision making from action (p. 1193).

Today there is general agreement that planning activities ought to involve people in most staffing categories.

In writing about program development at the Utah State Archives, Fagerlund (1990) discusses the involvement of employees in the planning group:

> Archives staff involvement was important for a number of reasons. They had valuable ideas and experience that contributed to the relevance, effectiveness, and feasibility of the plan. Participating in the evaluation and research gave staff an understanding of why things had to change and an acceptance that change was inevitable. Involvement gave archives staff members a sense of ownership of the new plan that was essential for implementation (p. 556)... The written plan creates a future vision that can unify and focus activity. It communicates to sponsors in an effective way and enables them to evaluate progress and provide support when needed, including the seizing of opportunities of which archival management may be unaware (p. 557).

Collaborative planning is a shared understanding of the work required for project completion. The people who implement a plan should help to prepare it—otherwise you risk uncommitted contributors, erroneous estimates, and overlooked tasks. People dislike being told how to do something, especially for a project that may lie outside their regular duties. Instead, you should use the team's knowledge to determine the best way for it to perform the work. Team members forming estimates have ownership of them. If the estimates are wrong, they will take steps to correct them and learn from the experience. Members are more likely to cooperate with your requests when they understand or agree with them. Developing the plan together ensures that the commitments are based on decisions that have been made by the contributors themselves.

You should avoid planning granularly at the start of the project, because there is a likelihood that the plan will change. A project manager can spend a considerable amount of time planning to the smallest detail, to the point that the plan becomes so rigid that it is difficult for the team to respond to unexpected events. It is impossible to know all contingencies and foresee every problem in the planning stages. However, teams can suffer from excessive flexibility, which can lead to *ad hoc* decision-making and lack of team cohesiveness, causing time and cost overruns.

As you plan, ask yourself various project questions (Table 4.2). Your responses lay the foundation of a project plan to build upon as you gather more information. Some of the techniques described in this book may seem unnecessary for small projects, when in some cases the team can accomplish processes more informally. Planning focuses on making sure that the project has a definite aim and enough support to achieve its purpose. Many projects flounder because they are set up to address issues that people feel are urgent, and the inclination to take action means that ideas and their consequences are not considered in their entirety. Rushing the initial thinking may fail to achieve objectives and add more delay. The time used to plan a project is always well spent.

The project plan will contain expressions of how expectations of quality, budget, and time are to be met. Project managers will calculate the right amount of money to deliver the specified products in the proposed timescale. The plan may fail to meet expectations in one or more respects,

Table 4.2 Project Planning Questions

- What is the purpose of the project?
- Who needs to be involved?
- What results will be produced?
- What constraints must be satisfied?
- What assumptions are being made?
- What work has to be done?
- When does each activity start and end?
- Who will perform the work?
- What other resources will be needed?
- When will the project be done?
- How much time will it take?
- How much money will it cost?
- What are the risks? What could go wrong?
- What resources are needed? How will they be procured?
- Under what circumstances should the project be cancelled?

but any change in one aspect of the project constraints has an impact on another, so the process should be reapplied to any changes. In this way, the plan is refined to a point at which it satisfies as many stakeholders' expectations as possible.

Your project description must show how the project will solve the problem you have identified. You need to demonstrate that the planned activities, the number and types of staff, and the timeframes are realistic. The project you have designed should seem to have a reasonable chance of succeeding in achieving its objectives.

When developing the plan, avoid assigning aggressive start and finish dates without sound reasoning. Although it is usually better to pursue a schedule that completes the project quickly, compare the benefits of speed with its risks and potential consequences.

Fortunately, many projects are not time-critical. Few organizations are impacted critically if the schedule slips. Occasionally, a deadline is arbitrarily established to motivate the team; it is an illusion. Keep that in mind while scheduling. As a project manager, question and push back on deadlines that seem unrealistic.

A common mistake for project managers is backward scheduling. Senior management sometimes mandate a deadline for the project; project managers start with the end date and more backward into the schedule for the preceding work. The error is that these dates leading up to project completion are invalid. With backward scheduling, the project team undermines the planning process by accepting the entire scope of the project with a definitive deadline. When a project has a fixed end date, there is a tendency to try to compress the schedule to fit everything into the time available. Too often, it becomes apparent that the schedule is impossible. Be realistic at the outset about what can be delivered and what cannot. Productive time may only amount to four days a week, and meetings, communication, and coordination need to be integrated into the schedule. Allow extra time for contingencies such as unpredictable interruptions.

A far more successful endeavor is to plan the date your project ends; do not let the date plan your project. Planning should take place to determine what the team can accomplish within the period and resources available to the organization. A firm end date determined by your schedule creates a sense of responsibility for the project, gives the team something to work toward, and confirms that the project will conclude without dragging on indefinitely.

When scheduling, be practical with the days allotted to complete each aspect of the project. Build in flexibility to allow for staff absences, holidays, and delays. A good benchmark is to build in 10% extra for each step of the process.

If a project takes place over the winter, plan to have less work done in December. This time can be used as a buffer to be consumed if the project falls behind schedule. People are motivated to catch up on their work if there is a realistic expectation that it is doable. By planning for the inevitable slowdown that occurs during the holidays, you have a built-in period during which the team can get back on schedule without Herculean efforts.

Sometimes the team may have to work during the holidays. At this time, scrutinize your schedule and determine if the team needs to work through the holiday break. If you are working on a project with an international team, remember to check the date of holidays in the other countries and schedule accordingly.

4.2 DEVELOPING THE WORK BREAKDOWN STRUCTURE

A work breakdown structure (WBS) is a deliverable-oriented hierarchy of the tasks that must be performed to accomplish the objectives of a project. It has many benefits (Table 4.3). A WBS facilitates buy-in to the project scope and the effort involved by the stakeholders. It identifies required work for the project, and reduces the number of items that are forgotten. It allows each team member to understand how his or her work fits in the project and how tasks impact the work of others. It provides a basis for cost, time, and resource needs, as well as the decisions made for the project. A well-crafted WBS can be used as a template for similar projects in the future.

A WBS is a foundation for estimating work, choosing resources, building a project schedule, and tracking progress. At its highest level, the WBS conveys a strategy, a methodology, and the best practices regularly used in your project. At its lowest level of detail, a WBS expresses unique work packages that must be performed. A work package is a collective name given to a project task and all its relevant work information. Included in this package are the task name, schedule start and end dates, duration, effort estimate, deliverables, completion measurements, quality measurements, and standards.

If done well, the WBS prevents omitted deliverables, gains the commitment of project personnel, enables the development of a project

Table 4.3 Work Breakdown Structure Benefits

- Understanding the work at early stages
- Avoiding uncontrolled changes
- Delivering what is expected
- Understanding areas with limited knowledge
- Estimating costs
- Visualizing internal and external work
- Envisioning project boundaries
- Managing complexities
- Providing a baseline for scope change control
- Assigning and explaining the work
- Enhancing project planning
- Avoiding replanning
- Detecting early warnings for problems
- Improving communications
- Achieving a shared understanding of the work
- Improving project reporting
- Gaining stakeholder buy-in
- Monitoring, measuring, and controlling work
- Inspiring confidence and gaining credibility
- Integrating scope with time and cost
- Improving future projects

plan, and reduces risk. It outlines the work to be performed in a logical way and makes progress easy to track.

A WBS must be performed in a systematic fashion so that there is a logical pattern to the breakdown. The most efficient way to build them is to think the project through from start to finish, asking along the way, "Who does what?" To begin, utilize the scope statement and deliverables to identify the top-level tasks, and then split the work that constitutes each task. Intermediate deliverables assist in identifying lower-level summary tasks and work packages. A WBS is constructed with two or three levels of detail, although more levels may be required for complex projects. A WBS task template may be found in Appendix E. Different parts of a project might require diverse levels of decomposition. One project section might include more work, so you can break it down into three levels; if another part of the project is simple, you may need only two levels.

Small teams of people can tackle different areas of a WBS. A management team might work on the high-level WBS while the project team might flesh out the lower levels and work packages. Start by identifying the logical subdivisions of the project, and then break each of these down further. The goal of a WBS is to determine a unit of work that is discrete and advances the project toward its completion.

Involve the people who will have to do the work, because they will know what is involved in each job and how those jobs can be made into manageable pieces. The project manager and team members should analyze all tasks to determine if they are necessary and whether some can be redesigned to make them faster or cheaper to complete. Check your work by reviewing the subtasks and determining whether they combine into the highest-level tasks.

How much itemization is appropriate? One approach is to match the project work to the frequency of your status reports, so you have measurable progress for every report. Try to create work packages using the 8/80 rule. The smallest item in the scope decomposition should take more than eight hours of labor but fewer than 80 hours to create. This prevents requirements packages from being too large or too small to manage.

A WBS enables you to estimate how long each activity will take. You might need to make inquiries before you determine if the work requires delivery of materials or time to complete processes. Spend time to try to make the estimate as accurate as possible at this planning stage, because the schedule will be based on this information.

Your WBS may reveal some challenging conclusions: the project may cost more than it is worth, the organization lacks the skills to do the job, or it will take too long to complete. These revelations should make management think twice before proceeding. Doing the work to develop the WBS will reveal these critical details.

4.3 DEFINING THE SEQUENCE OF WORK

The WBS does not show the sequence in which work is performed: such sequencing is determined when a schedule is developed. In some projects, certain tasks are the foundations for others and have to be completed first. Activity sequencing establishes logical relationships, known as dependencies, between project activities. Dependency is defined as one task that is dependent on another being completed before it can begin. Dependency is important in planning a project because it can be costly. For example, staff time is wasted if people are available but cannot start work until others have completed their tasks. Delays happen if estimates of how long the earlier tasks will take prove to be incorrect. Determining specific tasks can help define the sequence of work, and there are guidelines available (Table 4.4) to help you do this.

Table 4.4 Guidelines for Determining Tasks

- If a task will take longer than two weeks, split it.
- If a task involves a number of people, break it into several tasks.
- If it makes sense to make one person accountable for a part of the task, separate it.
- If a task spans a major checkpoint, such as a progress meeting, divide it just before the checkpoint.
- If a task produces several different products, separate it.
- If a task consists of an activity, a waiting period, and an activity, split it.
- If a task produces a series of components that require quality testing, divide it.
- If a task contains a number of dependencies, break it into several tasks and allow some contingency for delays.

Vivid LAM example

There are three types of dependency. Mandatory dependencies use hard logic—for example, shelving in an archives needs to be installed before boxes can be shifted to the shelving. Discretionary dependencies use soft or preferred logic. For instance, you typically paint the walls of a new library annex before you lay flooring; however, if the painter is on another project, you can choose to install the flooring first and have the painting done later after the flooring has been protected. Any time you bypass preferred logic, you must also account for the risk that will be added to the task. Finally, external dependencies determine when you can schedule some activities—for example, if you are updating your website with materials from your museum collection, you have to coordinate your efforts with the digitization vendor which is handling scanning of the materials.

Dependencies between tasks have defined relationships. In most cases, one activity cannot start until another action is finished. This is referred to as a finish-to-start relationship, and it is the most common form. However, there are four ways in which several activities can depend on each other (Table 4.5).

A network diagram displays the sequence in which activities will be performed; its basis is the WBS. Since not all activities can be performed simultaneously, the technique determines the logical sequence of work and documents the dependency relationships between activities and work packages. Figure 4.1 shows a sample network diagram. In a network diagram, the nodes represent the activities of the project, and the arrows signify the milestones or deliverables from each activity. Project managers create a network diagram using the precedence diagramming method. This is referred to as activity on node, because it shows the activities in nodes, with

Table 4.5 Task Dependencies

- Finish to start: Task 1 must end before Task 2 can start. This is the most common relationship. For example, design for a new archival website must be completed before building it can begin.
- Start to start: Task 1 must start before Task 2 can start. While it sometimes happens that both tasks start at the same time, this is not always the case. For example, setting up interviews for special collections catalogers must start before the interviews can start.
- Finish to finish: Task 1 must finish before Task 2 can finish. This relationship links tasks that can be worked in parallel, but one cannot finish until the other does. While both tasks sometimes end at the same time, this is not always the case. For example, testing a new book checkout system cannot be completed until programming has finished.
- Start to finish: Task 1 must start before Task 2 can finish. This is the least common dependency. For example, delivering a digitization project's results must start before paying the final invoice to the digitizing vendor can finish.

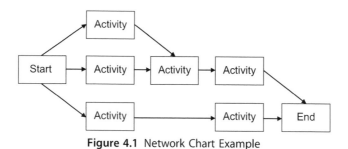

Figure 4.1 Network Chart Example

arrows representing dependencies between activities and the sequence in which they will be performed.

Examining network logic and dependency relationships can validate the project's WBS. Conversely, when your team begins to define predecessors for activities, you may discover that current activities need to be modified to make the logic work or that activities or work packages need to be added to the WBS.

Within the project there are phases, or a portion of the project that must be completed before the next phase can begin. Phases make up the project life cycle, and the completion of a phase usually creates a milestone that shows progress in the project. Phases do not overlap each other in execution, but it is possible that they could overlap to save time or if the nature of the project work allowed phases to happen in unison.

Whenever possible, avoid using dates for tasks unless they are required. The reason for circumventing date constraints is because they signify that a task must happen on a date regardless of the completion of tasks before or after it. The best method of assigning a task is to assign a time period in which it must be performed, and then predict when the task may happen based on the best- and worst-case scenarios for the predecessor tasks' completion.

4.4 DEVELOPING THE SCHEDULE

By coalescing information on the preferred sequence of tasks, their estimated durations, and the assumed project start date, you reveal the total project duration and the expected project completion date, which will determine your schedule. A schedule is so much more than a list of tasks and assignments: it is the heart of the project plan. Schedules allow for commitments to be made, encourage everyone to see their work as a contribution to a whole, and enable progress tracking. When schedules slip, they still have value. A project schedule can help you plan for risk, adjust for tasks finishing early or late, and communicate effectively with your team. It contains the activities to be performed and their order, and consists of several components (Table 4.6).

Managing a project schedule is something the project manager works on over most of the life of the project. The schedule is fine-tuned as more is learned about the project. During this adjustment, consider risks. Alterations, like shortening a schedule to meet deadlines, adding resources, or making other changes, introduce risk to the project. Revise your risk management plan as you build your schedule.

The path to schedule development includes defining activities, arranging the activities in order, and estimating the resources required to complete them. There are several project schedule methods available for project managers (Table 4.7).

Table 4.6 Schedule Components

- Project activities
- Person responsible for each task
- Duration of each action
- Predecessor activities
- Successor activities
- Resources required to accomplish each activity
- Start and end dates of each activity

Table 4.7 Project Schedule Methods

Method	Attributes	Benefits	Notes
Calendar	Microsoft Outlook and Google Calendar allow teams to share calendars	Employs software that is easily available and familiar to everyone	Use only for small projects
Gantt chart	A bar chart that shows various WBS levels	Easy to understand, incorporates the WBS, and shows progress against estimates	Does not present interdependencies
Milestone chart	A bar chart that shows start and end dates, deliverables, and external dependencies	Highlights decision and completion points	Milestone tables are also used but without bars
Network diagram	Uses nodes and arrows, with dates added to each activity node	Highlights the critical path and shows the flow of the project	Best suited for wall display

One simple yet effective way to track task completion dates is to use the calendar software most of us have on our computers, such as Microsoft Outlook or Google Calendar. Project managers can add tasks to the calendar, share calendars with other team members, add reminders for tasks, and copy and paste information to other software programs for report preparation. This approach may be unsuitable for large, complex projects, but is ideal for smaller projects and especially for organizations that cannot afford scheduling software.

Large schedules should be divided into smaller plans to minimize risks and increase adjustments. Each task has to be assessed in terms of content, staff members needed, and time required; this allows you to make an initial estimate of the resources necessary. You might find that this estimate leads to the project taking longer than intended, in which case you may want to approximate time and resource costs for increased staffing to accelerate the accomplishment of the tasks. Schedule the project by taking into account the workloads of the team members, which might affect the start date and their capacity to perform the work. You can decide whether additional staff will be necessary or whether the tasks should be scheduled to allow work already committed to be completed first.

The objective when planning is to determine the shortest time necessary to complete the project. Begin with the WBS and determine the time required to complete each subunit. Next, determine the sequence in which the subunits must be completed, and which may be happening at the same time. This analysis will identify the three most significant time elements: the duration of each task, the earliest time at which a step may be started, and the latest time at which an action must be started. Several schedule constraints should be examined (Table 4.8). These determine when and why a project must start or finish.

The most commonly used scheduling technique is the Gantt chart, named after the management consultant Henry L. Gantt (1861–1919). During World War I Gantt worked with the US Army to portray the status of the munitions program visually. He realized that time was the common denominator to most elements of a plan, and that progress could be assessed by viewing each element's status with respect to time. He recognized that the process could be broken down into precise phases and that many phases could be executed concurrently, in whole or in part. He organized processes with this in mind, so the schedule's efficiency could be maximized. His approach used standardized setup and processing times and depicted the relationship between tasks planned and completed, represented in a bar chart

Table 4.8 Schedule Constraints

- As soon as possible (ASAP): A task will transpire as soon as it can. It is the default when assigning tasks from the start date. This is a flexible constraint.
- As late as possible (ALAP): A task will occur as late as possible without delaying dependent tasks. It is the default when assigning tasks from the end date. This is a flexible constraint.
- Start no earlier than (SNET): A task will begin on or after a particular date. This is a semi-flexible constraint.
- Start no later than (SNLT): A task will commence by a specific date at the latest. This is a semi-flexible constraint.
- Finish no earlier than (FNET): A task will be completed on or before this date. This is a semi-flexible constraint.
- Must start on (MSO): A task will begin on a specific date. This is an inflexible constraint.
- Must finish on (MFO): A task must be completed by a particular date. This is an inflexible and deadline-oriented constraint.

	Jul	Aug	Sept	Oct	Nov	Dec	Jan	Feb
Identify research area	▓							
Formulate research questions		▓						
Select research methods and design		▓						
Write proposal			▓					
Negotiate access			▓					
Conduct literature review			▓	▓	▓			·
Collect data				▓	▓			
Analyze data					▓	▓		
Write first draft						▓	▓	
Receive feedback							▓	
Write final draft								▓
Submit report								▓

Figure 4.2 Gantt Chart Example

which came to be called the Gantt chart. One of its major strengths is that it can be used in the management of both simple and complex projects. The Gantt chart became widely adopted, and today is utilized in various ways.

The chart consists of a horizontal scale divided into time units (days, weeks, or months) and a vertical scale showing project work elements (tasks, activities, or work packages). Figure 4.2 shows an example of a Gantt chart for a research project at a museum. To create a Gantt chart, list the steps required to complete a project and estimate the time necessary for each step. List the steps down the left side of the chart and time intervals along the bottom. Draw a line across the chart for each step, starting with the planned start date and ending on the completion date of that action.

Some steps can be performed at the same time, with one taking longer than another. Planning allows some flexibility about when to start the shorter step, as long as the plan has it finished in time to flow into subsequent steps. This situation can be represented by a dotted line continuing to the time when the step must be completed.

Your Gantt chart will show the minimum total time for the project, the sequence of steps, and which steps can be ongoing simultaneously. You can maximize the usefulness of a Gantt chart by plotting progress: draw a line in a different color below the original line to show the actual beginning and ending dates of each step. Doing so allows you to assess whether or not the project is on schedule.

Preparation of a Gantt chart occurs after a WBS analysis and identification of work packages or other tasks. During WBS analysis, the functional manager or others responsible for a work package estimate its time and prerequisites. The work elements are listed in time sequence, taking into account that some elements must be completed before others can be started. Each work package or tasks for the WBS should appear as a scheduled activity on the Gantt chart.

Gantt charts are limited in their capacity to show activity inter-dependencies—in other words, they cannot show the logical relationships between activities because they are time-based diagrams. In projects where the steps flow in a simple sequence of events, Gantt charts can portray adequate information for project management. However, when several steps are in progress at the same time and a high level of inter-dependency exists between the various steps, project evaluation and review technique (PERT) diagrams are a better choice. These diagrams reveal the logical relationships between a project's activities to help the project manager and team design the best sequence of tasks for completing the project.

Developed during the 1950s by the US Department of Defense, PERT diagrams help identify the critical path and establish the earliest and latest start and finish times, duration, and floats. The protocol emerged from the design process for the Polaris missile program, which involved many subcontractors and thousands of parts.

The PERT method was developed for projects where activity durations are uncertain. Projects like this are contracted while new developments are still unfolding, and before many of the problems in technology, materials, and processes have been identified. The project duration is uncertain, and a high risk exists that the project will overrun the target completion time.

PERT uses a network diagramming technique called activity on arrow, and an estimating technique called weighted averaging. The estimating portion of this technique is still used, although the critical path method (CPM) (discussed later in this chapter) has largely replaced the network diagramming portion. The advantage of network diagramming is in helping you find all the places where work can be done in parallel, thus creating the shortest possible schedule.

PERT diagrams have several components. Events are represented by circles or other closed figures. Arrows connecting the circles represent activities. A dummy activity has zero duration, and demonstrates a specific relationship and path of action on a network diagram. Dummy activities are useful to implement when the specific logical relationship between two particular activities cannot be linked. The dummy activity serves as a placeholder. When dummy activities are illustrated, a dashed line with an

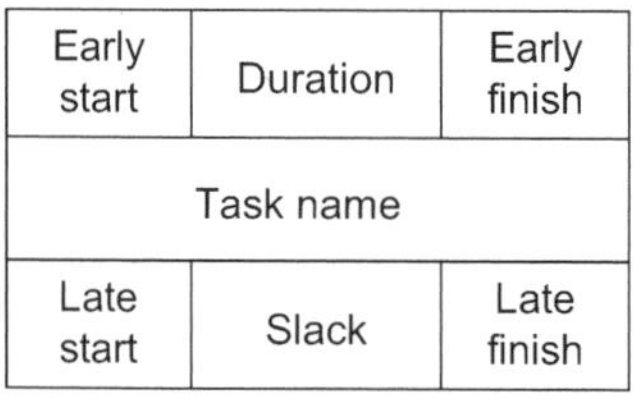

Early start	Duration	Early finish
Task name		
Late start	Slack	Late finish

Figure 4.3 PERT Chart Node

arrowhead on one end should represent them; they may be a different color than other activities.

PERT diagrams are most constructive if they show the time scheduled for completing an activity on the activity line. Time is recorded in a unit appropriate for the project, with days being the most common, and hours, weeks, or months occasionally used. Some diagrams show both high and low time estimates. Figure 4.3 is an example of a PERT chart node with various estimates.

The most sophisticated PERT diagrams are drawn on a time scale, with the horizontal projection of connecting arrows representing the amount of time required for each activity. In the process of diagramming to scale, some connecting arrows will be longer than the completion of that task requires. This discrepancy is slack time, and is depicted by a heavy dot at the end of the period, followed by a dotted-line arrow connecting with the following event.

Along with Gantt and PERT charts, several methodologies developed from software projects can be used to schedule projects. The waterfall method, for example, starts at the beginning of the project and continues in an uninterrupted manner until the end. Each phase in the waterfall has to be completed before the next step can start. The transition between phases is managed by gates, which represent the passage between one phase and the next. The gates are one way: once a gate has been passed, the project cannot return to the work that was being performed prior to moving through the gate.

The time-box method works for projects that are well defined. A time box is a method in which a task is broken into a series of more manageable chunks. Often it involves gathering together people engaged in the work and asking them to define short-range goals. Once the goals are reached, they are reappraised, and a new set of goals is identified.

The team defines a short-term time horizon, about one month, and set measurable objectives for the period. The team gathers and begins working toward the objectives. At the end of the time box, the result is assessed. If the objectives have not been achieved, set a new time box and begin the process again. The time horizon is defined by considering the task as a whole. Once you understand the task, you should break it into manageable portions that fit the time-box size for the task. All of the portions do not need to be planned; only the current time period needs to be.

An advantage of time boxing is the focus it provides. Instead of team members worrying about how to complete complicated tasks, they concentrate on short-term goals. This singlemindedness helps progress, since time is not spent on planning activities that are not understood.

The rolling-wave method is analogous to time boxing because it uses the same principle of splitting the work into different areas. The difference between the techniques is the focus of each box. In rolling wave there are two boxes: the first is approximately three months long and contains the detail of the work to be undertaken, and the other box is the rest of the project. The first part is practical, and the second is strategic. Beginning with the WBS and a master plan, create a master schedule and break your project into phases, typically 90 days each. Early on, plan the first phase in detail and future phases at a higher level. Midway into each stage, refine the next phase in detail. If the refinement causes a deviation from the promised time, cost, or scope, try to resolve the problem by overlapping tasks or adding resources. If that seems risky, negotiate trade-offs in scope, time, or cost with the project sponsor.

The rolling-wave method should be used on a project that lasts longer than a year. The method is applied at a higher level than time boxing, so it covers many activities, as opposed to time boxing, which covers only one activity. Rolling wave would typically be used at a higher level for the management of the project. It would not be used for the control of individual tasks within the project, which can be managed by time boxes.

4.5 EXECUTING THE PLAN

It is often difficult to start work on a project because your attention shifts from planning to action. When tasks are allocated and the scheduling is complete, team members will not automatically start working. The project manager ensures that work begins by making sure that everyone knows who should perform what tasks, and when each should start. Team members must be free to begin work, and the essential materials and equipment should be available. Even then, it is often necessary to urge your team to commence the project.

Implementation excites people managing projects because the planning turns into concrete outcomes. The work of a project manager changes from developing frameworks to monitoring activities to ensure that everything progresses as planned. The attention of those managing projects never strays from planning, because it keeps the balance between time, cost, and quality. Even when the implementation is about to start, a little more planning ensures that the transition from planning to activity is smooth.

A milestone chart presents a broad picture of a project's schedule and control dates. It lists critical events that are verifiable by others or require approval before the project can proceed. Because of its lack of detail, a milestone chart is unhelpful during the planning phase when more information is needed. However, it is particularly useful in the implementation phase because it provides a concise summary of the progress of the project. A project milestones template is given in Appendix E.

Work will be impeded if the necessary materials and equipment are unavailable or accommodation for the project has not been arranged. The project manager handles resource allocation and utilization, but if the resources can be linked to areas of responsibility, relevant budgets can be delegated to other members of staff in functional departments.

Some resources are required be managed by qualified people. If the project necessitates the handling of special equipment or materials, there may be statutes to observe. In setting up the project, identify people with particular qualifications or experience to manage these specialist areas of work.

Getting the appropriate resources for a project makes a significant difference. Working with fewer resources than you planned for or assigning people with less experience can delay the schedule. However, people, equipment, and materials are usually in short supply, so compromises are always a probability. The project plan should not just list resource names or generic skill sets—if you can delineate the skill sets you need, when, and for how long, it is easier to obtain resources or negotiate alternatives if the resources you want are unavailable.

You may work with a core team for initiating and planning, but executing the project is the time when you bring in the rest of the team and acquire the necessary equipment and materials. Procurement may be as easy as telling your team to start the project if team members come from within your organization.

4.6 PROCURING RESOURCES

Consider if your project may require results from other projects—or conversely, it may generate products that other projects can use, or address needs that similar projects have. You should identify projects related to yours as soon as possible so you can share personnel, coordinate resources, and minimize overlap in project activities and results. For resources beyond your organization, the procurement process includes solicitation, evaluation, selection, contracting, and ongoing management. Choosing a vendor requires negotiation and planning, as well as other skills (Table 4.9).

As part of your procurement, you should include a project procurement plan. You then have to review and approve the plan, define your selection criteria, identify potential vendors, create a statement of work (SOW), and create contract change processes.

For complex or competitive procurements, review the proposals, choose your preferred vendors, and arrange for demonstrations of their products if appropriate. Select your vendor, negotiate a contract, and update your schedule and project management plan if required. In addition,

Table 4.9 Tips for Choosing a Vendor

- Avoid meeting with salespeople who make unsolicited visits or calls. Although salespeople sometimes provide helpful information, they cannot tell you what you need for your project.
- Reject claims made either by salespeople or in promotional literature unless they are supported by product reviews in respected magazines and journals.
- Never feel obligated to purchase from a vendor.
- Avoid personal relationships, and decline favors from vendors.
- Check the vendor's references. Ask to see a list of organizations that made purchases.
- Ask the references about the vendors's accessibility after contracts were signed. Once the deal was complete, did they notice any changes?
- Include penalties in the contract for delays in equipment installation or services.
- Make the endpoint explicit in the contract, so it is easy to determine whether the vendor has met its obligations.
- Get the names of senior administrators in the chain of command so you can report problems to people empowered to solve them.
- Be clear about the cost. State in writing that costs are final, and no other charges will be added without your approval.
- Pay the full amount only when the project is finished and you are satisfied with the results. Pay less than 40% of the total cost up front.

you will want to allocate activities to monitor the procurement process throughout the project life cycle, such as maintaining relationships with vendors, reconciling invoices, monitoring delivery, and performing contract change control.

During the procurement of resources you may have to employ a request for information (RFI). This document enables you to obtain information from the suppliers which could provide the products and services you are seeking. Comparable to a fact-finding exercise, the RFI provides valuable information, such as which vendors can provide the services you need, pricing data, price comparisons, and identification of similar products and services. Contracts rarely come from an RFI, but releasing an RFI informs sellers that you might be procuring these products and services. It also means that you may issue a request for quotation (RFQ) or request for proposal (RFP) in the future.

An RFQ wants only a price from a vendor, and is typically released for straightforward purchases, such as buying scanners for an in-house digitization project. Using the RFQ, you should be able to select a supplier and sign a contract based on its response. It is slightly different from an invitation for bids, which implies that several vendors will be bidding on the opportunity to provide the goods or services.

Solicitation often starts with an RFP that asks vendors for bids. A proposal is used to procure products and services that are complicated, such as the construction of a building or the development of a software system. RFPs bring structure to the procurement decision-making process and enable project risks and benefits to be identified. They require the seller to provide information such as company history, financial stability, technical capability, and examples of similar project deliveries. An RFP contains the services you need, your schedule, and your budget. Include your vendor selection criteria, so companies can decide whether to bid. Provide instructions and the deadline for submitting a proposal, and the date you will announce your decision.

Once you have all the vendors' proposals, evaluate the responses using the criteria you have identified and determine which you would like to use. The selection process depends on the size and complexity of the project. Evaluation may be as easy as filling in a spreadsheet with ratings and choosing the vendor with the highest score. For large projects, you might reduce the submissions down to a shortlist of vendors and ask these in a second round to prepare a more detailed presentation. Some organizations require selection strictly based on the lowest bid; others evaluate each vendor's quality, reliability, and price. Some selection processes use complicated point systems for selection; others go with their gut feelings. As a consequence of the RFP, you should be able to select a vendor and sign a contract. Contracts are discussed in Chapter 5.

The SOW is the section of a contract that is created to establish what is expected from the vendor. It is often the same thing as a scope statement, discussed in Chapter 2. Regardless of the contract type you are using, SOWs should contain a detailed list of products and services to be procured, including the responsibilities of both you and the vendor, a deliverable schedule, a price structure, and a payment schedule. You may also include reporting metrics, incentives, penalties, acceptance criteria, and the warranty period. In some instances you can consider an SOW that contains characteristics of both the fixed-price and time-and-material contract types for different services.

4.7 KICKING OFF THE PROJECT

The project begins with a kick-off meeting, which is the first formal meeting of the project team members and stakeholders. An agenda should be prepared to keep things on track (Table 4.10). The meeting announces that the project is about to commence, communicates what it is about, develops expectations, and generates commitment to goals and deliverables.

Table 4.10 Typical Kickoff Meeting Agenda

- Introduction: Welcome the team and introduce everyone. Identify who will be involved in the project, and their roles and responsibilities.
- Executive perspective: Allow the sponsor to discuss why the project is important to the organization.
- Project initiation review: Hand out copies of the project charter and review it with the team. Ascertain that everyone is aligned with the project's purpose.
- Overview: Discuss the project's objectives, requirements, and deliverables.
- Approach: Elucidate on how the project will be undertaken. Explain the project phases and the specifics of the project itself.
- Schedule: Explain how the project will unfold, including major milestones.
- Team roles and responsibilities: Explain what elements the team members will work on and be ultimately responsible for.
- Communication plan: Clarify how and when future updates on the project's progress will be communicated.
- Plan moving forward: Determine the tasks that the team will be working on next. Identify whether or not any of the stakeholders' input will be required in the immediate future.
- Conclusion: Provide a summary of the meeting.

The meeting, led by the project manager, includes the stakeholders who will handle planning and executing the project—the project manager, assistant project managers for particular areas of knowledge, subject-matter experts, and functional leads.

The kick-off meeting happens somewhere between scoping the project and in-depth planning, which is the busiest time for a project manager across the entire lifespan of the project. The meeting should set the vision for the project. Everyone should recognize what this project is expected to achieve, why it is important, and where it stands in the organization's priority list.

Since the meeting sets the tone for the project, it is vital that everyone understands the goals, deliverables, and schedules. Even more important, however, is teambuilding. The meeting should take place in person: the cost of getting everyone together for a few days at the beginning of a project will be saved many times over by better communication and fewer conflicts. Shared experiences are the fastest ways to build rapport with and within a team.

The first day of the kick-off meeting should focus on introducing all the players, providing context to how the team and the project fit into the institution, and offering an overview of the project itself. Many organizations also invest in teambuilding activities.

On this day, you should welcome everyone aboard and make introductions. Acknowledge and thank all those who will contribute to the project. Mention each person by name. Many attendees will be core team members, while others will be peripheral members who participate in the project for a limited time. Share the meeting's goals, highlighting opportunities the project will present to the organization and to team members. You should also cover any unique aspects of the project that might present challenges beyond the ordinary.

Arrange for the sponsor to speak for 10–15 minutes on his or her perspective on the importance of the project. Support of senior management is a critical success factor for projects. Hearing from one of the organization's executives gives the project team a sense that the institution is behind the project. The sponsor's presence and behavior at the meeting are imperative to the project. Katzenbach and Smith (1993) write:

> When potential teams first gather, everyone monitors the signals given by others to confirm, suspend, or dispel assumptions and concerns. They pay particular attention to those in authority: the team leader and any executives who set up, oversee, or otherwise influence the team. And, as always, what such leaders do is more important than what they say. If a senior executive leaves the team kickoff to take a phone call ten minutes after the session has begun and he never returns, people get the message (p. 118).

The sponsor should explain why the project's work is important and how its goals align with the larger organizational objectives. Team members need to understand that they are part of something with important consequences for themselves and the organization; otherwise, they will not make their best effort. In larger organizations, political ramifications at the start of a new project may cause the sponsor to invite other senior managers so that they are aware of the project and its value to the organization.

On the second day of the meeting the project manager should establish the charter, identify major tasks and milestones, and ensure that everyone understands the scope and purpose of the project. Seek unanimous understanding of the charter. Engage people in discussion about the project, with the goal of reaching a consensus. Give an overview of the project that summarizes the business requirements and current plans for meeting those requirements. Ensure that the overview addresses the project charter, including any schedule or budget constraints.

Describe the resources available. Although you will want to stoke the team's enthusiasm at the kick-off, it is equally important to set expectations about the amount of support they will get. Describe team incentives. What, besides their regular compensation, will members receive if team goals are met or exceeded? If the team is unfamiliar with collaboration technologies, you may also need to train people on the program.

On the third day, once the project has been outlined and understood, you can begin assigning action items and due dates, identifying dependencies, and helping the team establish both formal and informal lines of communication.

4.8 MODIFYING THE SCHEDULE

All projects contain an element of uncertainty. Obstacles, some inevitable, can cause missed deadlines, cost overruns, and poor performance. Project managers must anticipate problems, replan activities, and shift resources as unforeseen problems occur. Carpenter (2010) warns, "Libraries, museums and archives are highly labour-intensive, with people as the main resource, [and] these two concepts of duration and effort are crucial to the effective scheduling of a project and need to be kept constantly under review by the project manager" (p. 29). Modifying the schedule is one way to solve problems when the project is delayed. There are several schedule

Table 4.11 Schedule Compression Techniques

Technique	Definition	Issues
Crashing	Adding resources to critical path activities only	Some activities cannot be completed faster by adding more workers; they often add overhead that negates any time savings.
Fast tracking	Performing critical path activities in parallel	This high-risk technique increases the likelihood of rework.
Process improvements	Increasing productivity based on different processes, technologies, and machinery	Process improvements are sometimes unavailable; new approaches may increase risks.
Overtime	Increasing the hours per day or per week available for project tasks	It is most useful when used for limited periods, as it may lead to decreased morale and work quality.

compression techniques, such as crashing, fast tracking, process improvement, and overtime (Table 4.11).

Execute phases simultaneously when possible, even if your original plan intended consecutive scheduling. Some phases must be organized and run consecutively—a later phase cannot start until the results of an earlier phase are available. In these instances, delays are troublesome since your team cannot proceed. However, in many cases you can begin a subsequent phase without completing a prior one.

Support your team's effort to absorb previous delays. A phase may be one team member's responsibility, but setbacks may make it impossible to complete it on schedule; you might be able to overcome the problem by assigning other team members to help.

Scheduling is done on the assumption that you will have the workers you initially planned on having or were promised. If someone is working on another project, or a team member will be used for several tasks, you may find that you have him or her overloaded. Scheduling software warns you that you have overscheduled your team and may be able to help solve the problem.

Begin preliminary steps for future phases to save time. You may be frustrated because delays are keeping your team idle. You cannot accelerate the phase under way or begin the next phase. However, you might be able to save time by partially completing upcoming phases. Some late phases in a project may be executed in a shorter timespan than originally scheduled. Doing this is the most likely way to make up delays created during earlier phases.

The critical path is a sequence of tasks that enable the completion of the project in the shortest possible time. It employs several definitions (Table 4.12). The critical path is the longest duration from project start to project completion. It identifies which tasks must be finished before others can follow. While some tasks can be sequenced with much flexibility, critical path tasks are confined to task relationships. The critical path is imperative when the project costs are significant, because scrupulous scheduling can ensure that the committed work days are as low as possible.

The CPM was created in the 1950s by DuPont to schedule renovations to its chemical plants. This technique uses a diagramming method called activity on node, and creates the project schedule based on the longest path through the network. The major difference between PERT charts and CPM diagrams is the graphic representation of tasks. Where the PERT chart uses activity on arrow and round nodes, CPM uses activity on node and rectangular nodes. This means that each node is a task. To show relationships, you draw arrows from predecessor to successor. This method of representation also enables us to model dependency relationships other than finish-start, which the PERT chart does not. Another difference

Table 4.12 Critical Path Definitions

- Duration: Number of work days, excluding holidays and other nonworking days, required to complete an activity.
- Forward pass: A strategy to develop early start and early finish dates for each task, starting at the beginning of the network and progressing to the end.
- Backward pass: A method to gauge late start and late finish dates by starting at project completion, using finish times, and working in reverse.
- Float or slack: The latest point a task may be postponed from its earliest start date without delaying the project finish date.
- Early start date: The earliest point an action can begin, based on the network logic and any schedule constraints.
- Early finish date: The earliest time the activity can finish.
- Late start date: The latest point that the action may begin without delaying the activity's successor.
- Late finish date: The latest point a task may be completed without hindering the activity's successor.

between the two systems is that PERT makes use of calculated task duration and allows you to estimate probabilities of complete work, whereas CPM just makes use of estimated task durations without regard for probabilities.

Determining the free and total slack for each activity helps project managers make schedule trade-offs. Free slack or free float is the length of time an activity can be postponed without delaying the early start of any following activities. The early start date for an activity is the earliest possible time it can start. Total slack or total float is the amount of time an activity may be deferred from its early start without delaying the planned project finish date.

You calculate free slack and total slack by performing a forward and backward pass through a network diagram. A forward pass establishes the early start and early finish dates for each activity. The early finish date for an activity is the earliest possible time it can finish. The project start date is equivalent to the early start date for the first network activity. Early start plus the duration of the first activity is equal to the early finish date of the first activity. It is also equal to the early start date of each subsequent activity. When an activity has multiple predecessors, its early start date is the latest of the early finish dates of those predecessors. A backward pass through the network diagram determines the late start and late finish dates for each activity. The late start date for an action is the latest possible time an activity might begin without delaying the project finish date. The late finish date for an activity is the latest possible time it can be completed without impeding the project finish date.

If the finish date is more important than the budget, spending money to shorten the schedule is an option; this is known as crashing. A common crashing technique is adding more workers to a task, which is a useful approach when used in a limited way. But if you add too many workers, the project slows as people get in each other's way. Other options include paying for overtime, paying rush fees for faster delivery of materials, and paying for people with higher rates who can hopefully complete work quicker.

Like any technique for shortening the schedule, the tasks you want to crash are on the critical path because they are the ones that determine the duration of the project. First, look for the longest tasks on the critical path. Crashing can increase the risk of those tasks, which is why the number of crash tasks should be kept to a minimum. Crashing one long task duration might cut all the time you need out of the schedule. By crashing longer tasks, you can crash fewer of them. After you have crashing candidates, evaluate these tasks to find the ones that are most cost effective.

When schedules have to be shortened, everyone on the team should be encouraged to make each day count. They should be sensitive to changes that increase the scope of the project. They should also raise alerts if they find themselves waiting for other people to complete their work or if they sense a delay. They should be encouraged to start and finish jobs early if they can do so without compromising quality.

Working overtime may be a way to bring the project back on schedule. Most team members will understand the occasional need to catch up on work, but ask for overtime only when needed. Not only does it increase the project cost when people are paid for overtime, but it may also lead to burnout—which, in turn, leads to a decrease in efficiency, defeating the purpose.

Additionally, there may be a need to balance the amount of work assigned to people on your team, such as lengthening, delaying, and splitting assignments, which will affect the schedule. Lengthening the duration of tasks and letting them run simultaneously can be helpful when a team member is overloaded because assignments are scheduled at the same time. When you increase the duration of tasks, the person works fewer hours on each assignment during the project. Delaying assignments is another way to balance a team member's workload, especially if someone has several work packages scheduled at the same time. Delays are ideal when assignments are short because it helps the person stay focused and productive. Splitting a longer assignment into smaller tasks is the third technique for leveling workload. This is a good solution when you need to include a brief, critical task in your schedule.

CHAPTER 5

Budgeting and Performance

There is measure in all things.

Horace

One machine can do the work of fifty ordinary men. No machine can do the work of one extraordinary man.

Elbert Hubbard, American writer

An ounce of performance is worth pounds of promises.

Mae West

5.1 DETERMINING THE BUDGET

A project should be completed without exceeding its authorized expenditures. In commercial projects, failure to complete work within budgeted costs may reduce profits and any expected return on the capital invested, with the risk of financial loss. Many projects, however, lack a direct profit motive, especially in archives, libraries, and museums. For these projects, even in the absence of monetary gain, careful attention to financial management is vital too.

Project managers need to know what a project costs. Accurate cost estimating is often difficult because it begins with the project's conception and before all necessary information about the project is available. You develop a budget in stages, from an initial estimate to a detailed estimate to an approved budget. Occasionally you may revise your budget while your project is in progress. The less defined the project, the less information exists and the greater the chances that the estimated costs will differ from the final numbers. The variance, unfortunately, is often on the side of a cost overrun.

Sometimes projects are so strongly supported by influential people within the organization that it is challenging to make an unbiased appraisal of them. Conflicting values and loyalties may exaggerate the anticipated benefits. Applying financial tests can help to ensure that the decisions made about investment in these projects will stand up against scrutiny.

As a project manager, it is your obligation to provide a valid project cost to the sponsor so that he or she can make a decision about whether

Project Management for Information Professionals
ISBN 978-0-08-100127-1

the project should be completed or not. Do not be intimidated into committing to a lower value than is possible. It is far wiser to present realistic costs than to underestimate costs and set yourself up for problems in the future.

When first determining the budget, consider the constraints. How much money is available? When should the project be completed? What internal resources are required? What external resources are needed, and what will they cost? What are you willing to settle for that will still meet your needs? Is there a way to complete the project using less expensive or fewer resources?

For large projects, such as the construction of a conservation lab or the development of a research institute, the project team should work with the organization's development office to begin fundraising efforts. The focus should be on the capital campaign, but the project manager should also push for endowments to pay for costs beyond the life of the project.

It is also helpful to review payment approaches and how they can influence your budget. Standard methods are payment upon delivery, payment on a schedule, payment on a schedule with variable payments, and payment on milestones when a predetermined piece of a deliverable is produced and verified.

Payment upon delivery is a straightforward approach. When you receive a product, you confirm its validity and acceptability. The vendor then submits an invoice on preagreed terms, such as payment due within 30 days. As project manager, you should have planned for the appropriate funds to be available from your budget to pay for the product.

Payment on a given schedule is also uncomplicated. This is the approach used when you are procuring workers on an ongoing time and materials basis. The outsourcing firm will take the hours claimed for your project and submit an invoice. You determine the accuracy of the hours worked, ensure you are getting the quality of work you expected, and confirm the validity of the invoice. These payments can also be planned by predicting the hours you expect to be billed in advance and including the budgeted amount in your project cost plan.

Payment on a regular schedule with variable payments is handled similarly to the previous approach, because scheduled sets of payments are to be made. The variable payment portion occurs when the amount of work required is based on a forecast. A base monthly fee is necessary for the service of handling orders, with a potential rebate or additional payment if the forecast volume varies from a given baseline workload. In this case, you plan the regularly scheduled payments and you watch how the workload volumes progress. Adjust your payment schedule quarterly.

Finally, the payment on milestone approach relates to your project schedule. Aspects of what you require your vendor or partner to do are delivered in parts that should be captured in your project schedule. Payment on each milestone is a fixed amount, so it is straightforward to include it in your budget. The verification of the deliverable against the milestone can sometimes take time, so the period to perform that task should be included in your schedule.

Your payment timing to vendors can affect your project costs and the financial state of your organization. Depending on the sizes of the purchases, they can have consequences for your budget. Your organization may direct you to delay buying something until the next accounting period. Conversely, it may want to you to spend money now rather than wait, so the budget allocation remains the same in the next fiscal year or quarter.

Given these circumstances, it is wise for you understand what flexibility you can apply to your project schedule to accommodate different pro-curement opportunities. You may receive price breaks from vendors if you pay up front. For example, organizations will often purchase computer hardware and software and require ongoing support. The initial investment covers the hardware/software delivery, license fees, and a year of mainte-nance. However, most organizations will want support for longer. Paying up front for the original purchase with five years of support typically means that a lower price can be negotiated. You can depreciate the hardware or software and cost of the support as an asset. Conversely, your organization will incur a greater cash outlay now rather than dispersing payments for support over the upcoming years. Vendors may provide an arrangement where you pay a portion of the agreed amount up front and make payments on a regular basis afterward.

5.2 CALCULATING COSTS

Projects have a range of possible costs to contemplate when calculating them (Table 5.1). Project costs are either developmental or operational. Development costs arise during a project, and include the staff and resources required to produce outputs. Operational costs are associated with main-taining or using the project outputs. When calculating costs, become familiar with accounting concepts (Table 5.2).

Table 5.1 Possible Project Costs

- Salaries
- Fringe benefits (taxes, health insurance, and pensions)
- Office space
- Equipment purchase, use, or rental
- Software
- Resources
- Telecommunications
- Postage and shipping
- Printing and photocopying
- Travel
- Hotel and per diem
- Office supplies and disposables
- Stipends
- Tuition
- Professional development registration fees and materials
- Subcontractors
- Website design, hosting, and maintenance
- Dissemination expenses
- Evaluation costs

Table 5.2 Accounting Concepts

Concept	Description
Variable costs	Costs that adjust in proportion to changes in an organization's activities.
Fixed costs	Costs that remain constant.
Direct costs	Costs that are traced to the direct production of goods or services.
Indirect costs	Costs that cannot be traced to the direct production of goods or services.
Working capital	An organization's assets with its liabilities subtracted.
Straight-line depreciation	A method of depreciation in which the purchase price is subtracted from the salvage value and then divided by the total estimated life in years.
Accelerated depreciation	A method of depreciation that allows for greater deductions in the earlier years of the life of an asset.
Life-cycle costing	Costs from each project phase when total investment costs are calculated.

Costs are either direct or indirect. Direct costs are expenditures benefiting and identifiable to projects. Direct costs may also be allocated direct costs, which provide for the research, design, development, or production needed to accomplish project requirements. Indirect costs are those that, under normal requirements for expenditures, do not directly contribute to the accomplishment of project requirements. Indirect costs are sometimes used synonymously with overload.

Costs may also be classified as labor or nonlabor. Labor costs are monies paid to employees. Such costs are expressed in hours or hourly fractions, to which direct labor rates are applied to get dollar values. Nonlabor costs are fees paid to vendors or subcontractors for purchased parts or services.

The value of a project may be hard to express in financial terms if it is about enhancing something that is already available, such as an improvement of a process. Sometimes, identifying potential savings in time or resources is easier. You may be able to express the value in terms of the benefit to users.

Two major factors need to be considered when building your budget: determining the level of detail you will manage, and how you will track personnel hours. Organizational culture and contracts determine the level of budget detail required. Contracts also dictate the level of project detail. You may not always work within a contract. When you do, however, the contract type you are working with will define your budget management behavior.

Contracts comprise a statement of work, terms and conditions, deliverables, deadlines, and costs. There are three main contract types: time and materials contracts, cost plus contracts, and fixed price contracts.

Time-and-materials contracts require spending to be tracked so they can be billed. These contracts are typically used for the purchase of services, not products. Most time-and-materials contracts have a fixed duration period, with an agreed amount to be paid per hour or per day. This type of contract is often used when the work cannot be specified and total costs cannot be reasonably estimated. With such a contract, you need to monitor project performance to ensure you are receiving value for your money and obtaining acceptable results in a timely fashion.

Cost-plus contracts are comparable to time-and-materials contracts. Costs are denoted to be billed, with the plus factor being a predetermined profit margin that is added above cost. With this contract type, the costs for work completed are reimbursed to the vendor, plus a fee representing a preagreed contribution to the vendor's profit. Incentives and penalties may exist for meeting or falling below the agreed costs, schedule, or other performance targets. A cost-plus contract is ideal to use when scope flexibility is desired, as you can redirect your vendor if the scope changes during the project. If you use cost-plus contracts when project risk is high, surprises may emerge that will need to be addressed with a more flexible contract model.

Fixed-price contracts may not dictate the same cost tracking structure, but you will want to note the spending against the revenue being generated by the contract. A fixed-price contract may not require the same details as a time-and-materials contract, but it is likely that cost elements like procurement or labor costs will be tracked.

With these contracts, the price is agreed up front for the products or services to be obtained. You must understand your needs and provide detailed information on what you want to procure. The vendor needs to be specific regarding the products and services it is offering. It is possible to establish financial incentives for meeting or exceeding agreed project milestones. In addition, penalties for missed milestones can occur. When creating a fixed-price contract, use both incentives and penalties to express a balanced perspective. Fixed-price contracts are best for projects with specific, known requirements.

Fixed-price contracts typically favor you as the buyer, as the vendor needs to commit to the fees up front for the scope of work. Smart vendors will include a risk-based contingency in their price to cover unexpected costs. Scope changes can be accommodated through a formal change management process. If a change is approved, the cost of the contract will increase and project documentation may be adjusted.

These are the most common contract types, although some organizations use other types. Cost-plus contracts are the most risky to use, because the vendor may waste resources without financial accountability. Fixed-price contracts are the most common and preferred. It is wise to have an attorney review the terms of contracts before signing them.

Another variable that can affect the way you monitor costs is your organization's model for tracking staff time. Some organizations, like consulting companies, record staff time carefully by using a profit and loss model and billing by the hour. You may be asked to track staff time against your project and your team members' tasks. Other organizations, such as most libraries, archives, and museums, consider internal staff to be a fundamental cost of doing business and may avoid tracking staff time against individual projects.

You may be asked only to track external resource costs like contractors. However, even if it is not required, tracking people's hours helps you validate current estimates and produce new ones that are more accurate. It can help you understand how much money and time are spent producing your deliverables. Additionally, if your project is a substantial part of someone else's budget, senior executives are likely to want some budget detail. They may not warn you in advance that they will require budget information.

Sometimes costs are hidden. It might be suggested that a project that does not require additional staff members does not have staffing expenditures; however, this is a false argument because employees have job descriptions and agreed areas of work. If they are asked to do something different from what they normally do, this represents a cost because you are employing the staff to accomplish different work. In some circumstances this is acceptable; in others, it might indicate that workloads are unmonitored.

When a project begins, the consequences of redirecting staff from their regular work to the project need to be considered. Assumptions about staff availability should be discussed at an early stage because it influences costs. Assumptions about the extent to which staff members may be asked to work on projects can also be an issue. Project work costs may be concealed in the budget because their work is partially devoted to projects.

Reviewing workload allocations ensures that the organization treats staff members fairly when they are asked to work on projects in addition to delivering their usual work outcomes. When several managers share claims on a staff member's time, pressure to achieve performance levels in several different areas of work can be intense without a mechanism for overseeing the individual's workload. Staff members can also be at risk when performance expectations are increased without support and resources to enable additional work to be performed.

There may be a risk to the organization if staff members are unavailable to do the day-to-day work for which they are employed. If staffing costs are not estimated, the cost of the project is inaccurate. Sometimes it is less costly to hire staff specifically for a project than to redeploy existing staff, especially if current staff would have to be trained in skills that the new employees already have. If training existing staff is preferred, the costs and staffing associated with training become another phase to incorporate into the project plan.

Personnel costs can be estimated by breaking down the project into tasks and working out requirements in terms of the necessary skills and the number of staff members needed to complete the task. Decide on the appropriate rates of pay. Project-based organizations have standard approaches and formulae to calculate personnel costs.

Project managers should avoid including extra or inflated costs in their budgets. Presenting unrealistic budget estimates to your sponsors is erroneous. A better way to manage this is to utilize overtly discussed contingency funds instead. It makes sense to add a contingency element to early cost estimates. As each stage is passed, it should be possible to reduce the contingency element, accounting for what has been learned during the project's progress and the reduced risks that remain ahead. Thus the contingency element is carefully assessed and is not a fund to be used for rescuing a troubled project. If you feel you need to add money to address potential risks, you should communicate the need for it. Detail when those contingency funds may be desired, and highlight the task areas where you wish to apply it.

5.3 UTILIZING ESTIMATION METHODS

Cost estimates help determine budgets. They become the baseline against which performance is evaluated. After the project begins, the rates of actual and estimated expenditures are compared as a measure of performance. Without realistic estimates, it is impossible to evaluate work efficiency or determine in advance how much the finished project will cost.

An estimate is an assessment of a probability of the time and resources required for the delivery of a project. Estimating is an essential part of budgeting. Unfortunately, as a whole, people tend to evaluate based on weak assumptions and predict outcomes for work based on the best possible set of circumstances. Estimating is always a guess. As in most guessing, your judgment can be improved by knowledge and experience, and by the use of tools and techniques that support decision-making.

You may have to go through the budget estimation process several times. Often three levels of accuracy exist. A rough estimate of $\pm50\%$ determines if it makes sense to pursue a project in the first place. As you get additional details, you can create estimates that are more accurate. A mid-range estimate is $\pm25\%$. When you complete a project phase or a pilot project, you can reestimate the next phase based on what you have learned. A detailed estimate takes the longest to develop, but should be close to your final numbers, $\pm10\%$. Being able to estimate within that range is ideal.

Estimates are more accurate and reliable when developed by functional departments which have been assigned responsibility for an activity. Their experience increases the reliability of an estimate and improves the quality of the planning process.

Several techniques are available for use in estimating project costs, and the project manager may use a combination of them throughout the project's life cycle (Table 5.3). These methods vary, but the purpose of the estimating process is to determine, within a desired degree of accuracy, the total cost to produce a deliverable. The difficulty of determining costs varies depending on the project's type, the experience level of the team, the resources needed, and whether similar projects can be used for comparison. The methods fall into two categories: those that may be used without reference to prior experience (top-down and bottom-up, Delphi technique, expert opinion, analogy, and phased) and those that require estimation data from previous projects (parametric, work distribution, and standard project).

Table 5.3 Estimation Types

Types	Characteristics
Analogous	Utilizes information from previous projects to create estimates.
Bottom–up	Begins at the lower level of the WBS to provide time and cost estimates.
Delphi technique	Experts anonymously reply to questionnaires and receive a statistical representation of the group's response. The process repeats until it reaches consensus.
Expert judgment	Needed due to various factors that influence durations.
Historical information	Using project files, databases, and team members to improve estimate accuracy.
Parametric	Uses historical data and statistical relationships to identify work units and the effort per work unit. Also called quantitative-based estimating.
Phased	Estimates the project by phase to decide whether to continue the project.
Top-down	Begins with the result and applies it to a new set of tasks. The estimator uses relevant components from previous projects for estimation.

Top-down and bottom-up estimating helps overcome the challenge of the future becoming more uncertain the further ahead you look. They are created at different points in a project's life cycle. A top-down assessment takes the whole project and applies an overall timescale and cost to it. Established on the eve of the project, the evaluation dissects time and costs, but it is unlikely to go into detail because, in the early days of the project, lasting detail will be unavailable. Despite this, the organization demands to know how long the project will take and how much it will cost. Given the high-level nature of a top-down evaluation, it is common to add a contingency to allow for whatever assumptions have been made.

A bottom-up technique refers to estimating costs by breaking the project down into elements: individual work packages and end-item components. Costs are calculated separately and then aggregated to derive the total project cost.

The two approaches can be combined so that well-defined parts of a project can be separated into work packages and estimated bottom-up, and other less-defined portions can be determined top-down. Work package costs can be determined by dividing the work into smaller elements and estimating the cost of each (bottom-up), or by making an estimate from an analogy (top-down). The bottom-up method provides better estimates than the top-down method, but requires more data and accurate task definitions. However, project managers can use top-down estimating as a reality check for the bottom-up method.

As each stage is completed, the process is repeated. As more information becomes known, the amount of contingency at each stage should be reduced, and confidence in the estimate for the end of the project should increase.

Named after the Oracle of Delphi, which the Greeks consulted before major undertakings, the Delphi technique seeks to develop a consensus on estimates through meetings, questionnaires, and surveys. The method was developed by the Rand Corporation in the 1940s to forecast the impact of technology on warfare.

Many projects have a specialist aspect to them, and project managers cannot be expected to be specialists in every facet. Project managers ask experts to state how much money would be needed for a project. When the replies are received, anonymous feedback is obtained. The experts are encouraged to revise their estimates in light of these other views. During this process, the range of the estimates should shrink as the experts pinpoint a figure. If an agreement is impossible, the average score can be used to obtain a more reliable estimate than might otherwise have been produced.

An expert opinion is an estimate supplied by an authority—someone who uses their experience and expertise to provide a reasonable approximation when lack of information precludes a more detailed cost analysis. Expert opinion should be limited to cost estimating during the planning phase, and for projects that are unique and for which there are no previous projects to compare.

The analogy technique compares the project, or aspects of it, with something similar so that estimates can be developed. This method can be used at any level: overall costs can be estimated from the costs of an analogous project, and task costs can be estimated from similar tasks. The cost of a similar project is analyzed and attuned for differences between it and the proposed project, taking into account factors such as time, scale, and complexity.

Phased estimates are frequently used when the project is large or is developing something new for the organization. In phased estimates, the near-term work is estimated with a high level of accuracy, between 5% and 15%, whereas future work is estimated with around 35% accuracy. Phased estimates are considered rolling-wave estimates and reflect that the known variables occur in the present moment and future estimates will be decided later. Rolling-wave scheduling is discussed in Chapter 4.

Some types of projects are repeated within organizations. Much of the activity is repetitive every time a project is undertaken, so it would be prudent to use these experiences to improve future estimates. The work distribution technique relies on data gathered from previous projects, which it allocates across the standard project life cycle to arrive at the proportions of effort or budget required by each life stage.

Parametric estimating is a technique that utilizes the statistical relationship between historical data and other variables, such as the number of lines of code in a software application. This information is implemented for the purposes of calculating an estimate for the activity parameters. Higher levels of accuracy can be part of parametric estimating depending on how sophisticated the original data was.

The success of such a model depends on the reliability of data from previous projects and the projects themselves being similar. If such data can be recorded and improved over time, the model can be used flexibly. For instance, if a budget has been reserved, it is a straightforward task to distribute it across the stages of a project to get some sense of the amounts available for each. Alternatively, if the completed first stage used a certain amount of the budget, the amounts for the future stages can be calculated.

The standard project method depends on data from previous projects. A table is drawn up that applies two measures of the project so that an estimate of costs can be calculated.

When giving estimates to stakeholders, make sure they are aware of all the assumptions and variables built into those calculations. Consider presenting cost factors as ranges instead of fixed estimates. Any estimate is bound to be wrong; a range, on the other hand, is more likely to be right, because it accounts for variations.

Sometimes a not-to-exceed figure may work even better. Everyone can focus on that number, rather than on a range where the sponsor and executives are likely to remember the estimate on the low end while you note the estimate on the high end.

5.4 EXAMINING THE COST OF QUALITY

Quality refers to the degree to which the objectives and a set of characteristics of the deliverables fulfilled the requirements. It is measured by whether the project meets or exceeds expectations. The expectations, of course, are the deliverables, services, or results the user will receive throughout the project. You must define the quality metrics, provide quantitative measurements that will equate to quality, and explain to stakeholders what the measurements mean and how they will map to the requirements for quality acceptance within the project.

Quality is associated with deliverables and the management of project work. Deliverable quality infers fitness of the tangible output to be utilized by end users. This should be measured, but user expectations and experiences will ultimately determine quality. Quality is more than just balancing the scope, time, and cost of a project; it is conformance to project requirements.

Quality applied to the work of the project infers continuous improvement of how the project is planned, executed, and controlled. The focus is how well the project management process works and how it can be improved. Continuous quality improvement and process quality management are the tools used to measure process quality. One way to improve the quality of the outcome of any project is to improve the processes used to generate that result. Continuous process improvement enhances the efficiency and effectiveness of the processes by minimizing unnecessary activities and duplication of efforts. When we improve the quality of our processes, we work smarter and do a better job, completing more in less time for less money. By focusing on the quality of our work processes, we increase the scope that we can deliver, improve the quality of results, and reduce time and costs as well.

Quality is planned instead of expected. In the long term, the cost of planning and implementing quality is less than the cost of investigating and fixing quality problems and living with the consequences of poor quality. You achieve quality by planning it into the project, rather than examining the results of sloppy work and fixing the problems later. It is more cost-effective to do the work properly the first time. One fundamental quality requirement for a project is to complete it on time, with a full scope, and within budget—that is, to implement the schedule, scope, and cost baselines.

A project quality plan is a set of actions defined at the onset of a project that will produce quality results during the execution of the project. Work with stakeholders to establish acceptance criteria for each of the deliverables you produce. The plan identifies the standards that will be used on the project and how you will examine the work to ensure that quality exists within the project deliverables. It includes performing quality actions such as peer reviews by using various quality resources—for example, templates, standards, and checklists available within your organization.

Quality assurance procedures should be established early so that measures for monitoring can be communicated throughout the project (Table 5.4). Quality assurance examines the quality requirements of the project, inspects the results of quality control, and ensures that the project is using the correct quality standards. If a project is involved, documentation may include a quality manual that describes project aims and how each part of the project is organized, procedural documentation that states how tasks are to be completed, and relevant technical specifications.

Table 5.4 Quality Assurance Techniques

Technique	Description
Benchmarking	Evaluates similar projects to determine feasibility
Cost/benefit analysis	Compares the project's expenses to its benefits
Cost of quality	Determines the expenditures to maintain quality standards
Design of experiments	Shows the elements that affect project outcomes
Flowcharting	Uses cause-and-effect diagrams to display where problems occur

The cost of quality is the sum of all the costs to achieve the expected quality the user demands in the deliverables. It is the resources invested in training, safety requirements, and complying with laws and regulations, and steps added to ensure quality acceptance. This includes all the work to conform to the quality requirements and the expense incurred from nonconformance. The costs of nonconformance are rework, downtime, and waste. If you discover any processes that are producing below-quality products, you will need to change the methods. If you discover any defects, you will need to correct these, either by fixing the problems or by doing the work again without error.

5.5 EVALUATING PERFORMANCE

Project management regularly involves gathering data on project performance, comparing actual performance to premeditated performance, and taking action immediately if needed. Data on actual performance includes the time that activities were started and finished, the costs expended and committed, and the earned value of the work completed. This process must occur recurrently throughout the project.

Performance-based management involves establishing, managing, measuring, and evaluating performance data. Performance measurement systems should enable a project manager to monitor the project closely and enact changes. Developing performance measures for a project involves creating measures at the individual, team, and project levels, as well as creating policies and the operational framework to ensure that high-quality performance data is generated.

One proven way to evaluate performance is to use earned-value analysis. It was developed in the 1960s to allow the government to decide whether a contractor should receive a progress payment for work done. The method has become popular beyond government projects, and it is considered the correct way to monitor and control almost any project.

Earned-value analysis is a project management methodology that integrates scope, time, and cost to measure current project performance and forecast future performance. It evaluates how much a project is worth based on work that has been completed, using various calculations and ratios to measure and report on the status and effectiveness of project work. When differences that result in cost changes are discovered (including variances in cost and schedule), these changes are managed using the project's change control process. The function of this analysis technique is to document the cause of the variance, measure its impact, and determine whether corrective action should be implemented.

Although earned-value calculations are usually done by computer, it is important to understand the basis of each calculation and what it means. For example, suppose half of your project's duration has passed and half the budget has been spent. If only a quarter of the work is complete, the project is possibly in peril. You have to finish three-quarters of the work, but with only half the time and money left. Earned-value analysis can uncover problems like this because of the way it looks at work and cost over time. It presents the schedule and budget in monetary terms, allowing the project manager to view all aspects of project performance in the same units.

However, earned-value analysis needs to be put into context. Many projects have start-up costs, such as equipment purchases, so you would expect to spend more at the beginning than toward the end. At other times the work may change direction and, as a result, the project will improve, but it may make the project seem like it is fairing poorly when earned-value analysis is applied to it.

Some terms and formulae are associated with earned-value techniques (Table 5.5). The intricacies of determining earned value are beyond the scope of this book, but resources to learn more about it can be found in Appendix B. For our purposes, however, we will stay at the conceptual level.

Earned-value analysis is based on three calculations. First, you measure planned value, which is how much you plan to spend to complete the work scheduled through to the status date. It is the integration of cost and time or, more commonly, work hours and time that forms the baseline plan.

Table 5.5 Earned Value Terms and Formulas

Terms	Formulae
Budget at completion	BAC
Planned value	PV
Percentage complete	PC
Earned value	$EV = PC \times BAC$
Actual value	AV
Estimate at completion	$EAC = (AV/EV) \times BAC$
Schedule variance	$SV = EV - PV$
Cost variance	$CV = EV - AV$
Cost performance index (CPI)	$CPI = EV/AV$

It involves an estimation of how much a project will cost and a measure of what you expect to accomplish. Specifically, it uses the original cost estimates for activities to chart the cost or value of the work that you plan to get done over that time. Secondly, earned value is the amount of money you have earned by completing work. It is a gauge of the value of what you have accomplished. It charts the cost or value of the work you have gotten done at any point in time. The original activity-based cost estimates are used to perform these calculations. This is what is known as "earned value." The third measure is the actual value or the total expenditures for the project. It is what you paid for what you have accomplished. This is your actual cost expenditure at any point in time.

Keep track of the total, current, and remaining budget, as well as what was spent. At any time in the project you should know each of the following numbers to determine if your project costs are being managed effectively. The current variance is the difference between the current budget and the actual amount spent. The estimate to complete shows how much money will be needed to conclude the project; it is the amount you plan to spend from this point in time to the project's conclusion. The estimate to complete variance is the difference between the remaining budget and the estimate to complete forecast. This calculation delivers the costs incurred to date plus costs estimated for remaining work on the task. The estimate at completion is a prediction of what the total cost of the project will be given current performance factors; it is the actual amount spent plus the estimate to complete forecast. This calculation provides the costs incurred to date, plus costs estimated for remaining work on the task. The estimate at completion variance is the difference between the total budget for the project and the estimate at completion.

Other important values include budget at completion: the original cost estimate, indicating the funds required to complete the work. Percentage complete is a measure of the activities' performance and progress and is required for the earned-value calculation. Schedule value is a measure of the time deviation between the planned value and the earned value. It compares the actual project duration and the estimated duration. A negative number means you are behind schedule. Cost variance is a measure of the deviation between the earned value and the actual value of doing the work. You are over budget if you have a negative number. The cost performance index is used to calculate performance efficiency. Less than one means your project is costing more than you planned. Greater than one means you are using less money to do the project.

5.6 MAINTAINING CONTROL

The baseline is the latest version of the project plan. Benchmarks exist on all sides of the project triangle: time, cost, and scope. When discussed as a whole, they are often referred to as project performance baselines. Controlling and documenting changes to the baseline project plan is referred to as project change management.

Under the best circumstances, projects are completed on time, within a budget, and to the standards specified in the plans. In practice, projects involve a unique set of problems that create complexity and risk, such as project slowdowns. Table 5.6 outlines the ways in which projects can be modified to maintain cost, schedule, and quality. Plans change as work progresses, and each stage may have to be revisited before completion. Although projects have boundaries that protect them from other activities in the organization, external events will affect the project. A rapidly changing environment may have an impact on longer projects and may require the revision of plans and a realignment of objectives. In any project, issues emerge as events evolve. Project managers need to be aware of events that can affect the project plan, and should revise the plans if necessary.

Monitoring and controlling are related concepts: monitoring refers to watching activities, whereas controlling means taking action to continue or correct the course. Accordingly, project monitoring involves performance measurements and recommendations for corrective and preventive actions based on the variance of the measured performance from the planned performance, and controlling involves implementing the approved corrective actions.

Table 5.6 Tips on Modifying Projects

- Renegotiate with stakeholders. Can the budget be increased or the deadline be extended?
- Use contingency. Can you make up the work later?
- Narrow the project's scope. Can features be removed to reduce costs and save time?
- Deploy more resources. Can you put more people to work?
- Allow substitutions. Can you use a less expensive or more readily available item?
- Accept partial delivery. Can you receive the rest of the delivery later?
- Offer incentives. Can you provide enticements to facilitate the work?
- Demand compliance. Can you insist that people keep their promises? Use this tactic selectively to avoid damaging relationships in pursuit of your goal.

The plan itself is the crux of monitoring and control. If the plan fails to show all revisions, it will neglect the tools for monitoring.

It is challenging to pay attention to big-picture issues when you are immersed in a project. You lose touch with events occurring in the rest of the organization, because you have little time to think of anything other than the immediate pressures of the project. It is important to stay alert to changes in your organization because projects must move in the right direction. They should not do something that once seemed important but is now undesirable.

Various means are used to gather the information required to track project progress. Project status reports and meetings are formal reporting structures that enable you to collect information. Monitoring depends on the flow of information, so systems should be in place to get feedback on what is happening. However, monitoring is not a solitary activity accomplished by the project manager. If the project team is meeting to review progress, monitoring becomes dynamic and changes to the plan can be achieved by consensus. Involving the team helps keep everyone on target and builds commitment. However, if you rely on the impact of others, you may miss signs of difficulties. Project managers should make a point of checking in on the project to keep in touch with the daily realities that emerge as the work progresses.

Monitoring collects information about project progress and compares this information with the plan to identify any differences. It needs to be carried out routinely to determine any discrepancies between the plan and reality. To keep track of what is happening, gather information on two levels. The big-picture level includes objectives to which the project contributes and the balance of time, budget, and quality. The project activity level includes tracking individual tasks that have been initiated, are on schedule, or are due to be completed. Once the project manager identifies any differences, he or she can consider if there are issues. In some cases the variations will be within the tolerance that the plan allowed. If the progress of activities is different from the plan, you will need to take action. There is a danger that the project will miss its targets because progress is too slow, or if a delay in one activity will impact on others and cause further delay. Control may be regained either by taking action to change the progress or by revising the plan to accommodate the variation in the development of activities.

Monitoring progress enables the project team to detect problems quickly so they can make appropriate changes. Projects rarely operate as the team envisions them. Sometimes planning results in a smooth start-up with minimal problems, and the project team can launch activities according to the timeline outlined in the plan. In other situations the project team encounters setbacks and obstacles that delay the planned activities. When the project is delayed, the project manager and team members have an opportunity to review the plan to determine whether a reallocation of funds can resolve problems and allow the work to move forward. Regular monitoring and evaluation empower the project team so it can be aware of shifting circumstances, respond to them, and ensure a successful project.

Throughout the project, be on guard against scope creep or unwittingly conceding to pressure to do more than has originally been planned. Scope creep is the largest problem that most projects face. It refers to the way in which projects grow out of control. If change control is not exercised the project may be over budget, behind schedule, and inadequate, with little warning until it is too late.

Do not try to solve problems that lie beyond the scope of your project, even legitimate or urgent problems that your organization needs to address. It is okay to change the objectives midproject, but do so consciously, after making sure your stakeholders agree to the new objectives.

Control is about taking timely corrective action. As a project progresses, you will want to change things within the project's boundaries. Changes in the environment of the project will impact the activities that are part of the project itself. Whenever there is a decision to change the plan, record the changes so that a master plan is maintained. If you register changes, you will keep a living document as a basis for continued achievements.

Control depends on a stable scope. Failing to manage scope change is one of the most common reasons for loss of project control. When the scope is allowed to drift, the results are unfavorable. Control is achievable with a plan against which to measure progress. If the plan is unambiguous about what should be accomplished and when, it is possible to monitor progress correctly.

The control process manages significant change. Good project managers delegate, monitor, and report progress as a matter of course, making decisions regularly. Even so, overconfidence can be project manager's downfall. Small changes can have a lasting effect on a project. When added together, minute variances may become a critical mass that can affect the underlying justification of the project.

Slippage occurs when it takes longer than anticipated to complete particular tasks and thus it becomes impossible to adhere to the project schedule. Once the project manager has identified that the schedule is slipping and tasks may be late, there are different responses. Additional resources may be obtained. However, adding more staff may delay the project further. New team members will need training, and may take time away from the current project team. Introducing a small number of additional people sometimes produces benefits, often when they are given familiar or specific tasks.

A project manager can ask people to work harder or longer hours. In the short term, this strategy can work. If funding is available in the budget, paying some overtime is possible. However, used as a long-term solution, overtime can demotivate staff and lead to stress, burnout, and increases in sick leave or staff turnover.

You may also review the project and reduce its scope. Sometimes slippage can be dealt with by considering the scope of the project and either cutting some of the outcomes or postponing them until after the project has been completed.

Another response is to accept the slippage and renegotiate a new end date. Sometimes this is the most sensible course of action, as the implementation process often reveals blockages or problems that had not been anticipated at the planning stage.

5.7 REVIEWING COSTS

Cost control entails monitoring actual cost performance to identify and act on cost variances. It also includes vigorous control of changes to the project scope to prevent unnecessary cost increases.

A budget does not need to be evenly distributed across your schedule. You need to know if you are falling behind whatever pace you have set for the project. Create a system by which you will monitor your budget as the project proceeds. This includes invoices paid as well as expenses that have been agreed upon but not paid.

Ensuring that team members inform you on financial commitments is just as important as tracking actual costs. Have team members keep records of their expenses and any vendors which are still to be paid. It is easy to maintain control over the budget if you limit the number of people who spend money or make financial agreements. Everyone operating under the budget should understand the ramifications of spending more than their budget allows.

Depending on the nature of the project and your organization, you may have a system developed that allows each team member to set an amount within which to handle his or her tasks. They are expected to stay at or below that total. Alternatively you may have a centralized budget, with each person needing to get approval from you before making any financial commitments.

When the project manager finds that the cost schedule is not being followed, he or she must be able to take actions to maintain the agreed-upon cost schedule and document cost changes that occur during the project. The project manager must also have a strategy to deal with the need to ensure adequate financing for many years if the project is to be funded from annual or multiple appropriations.

Not every cost overrun is serious. Sometimes expenses run ahead of the plan because work is progressing more quickly than anticipated. On other occasions you may have underestimated the cost of a one-time item of expenditure, but feel this is likely to be offset by an overestimate elsewhere. The point at which even a minor overspend should be taken seriously is when it is an early warning that you have underestimated activities upon which the project is contingent.

Monitor expenditures to ensure that they are matching the budgeted amounts. Be ready to explain why extra costs are unavoidable. Common reasons that occur in projects include increased overtime to keep things on schedule, consultant fees to resolve unforeseen problems, and fluctuations in currency exchange rates for international projects.

Inevitably, there will be decisions that need to be addressed throughout the life of the project. Unforeseen circumstances may mean spending extra money. Tell the sponsor as soon as you perceive that unexpected expenses may require an increase in the overall project budget. If the budget is fixed, identify any nonessential features you can remove from the scope to bring costs back in line. Look for an area of the project where you can cut costs early on, because it may provide emergency funds when they are needed.

As prices fluctuate, project managers and senior executives must agree on a budget tolerance level. Depending on the project and its budget, the variance may be as little as 1% or as large as 10%. Do not use the range of variation as an additional cushion for your purchases, because the percentage you spend now may be needed later in the project. Any budget variance can be unsettling, as it may reflect a lack of planning, but typically senior management is more eager to deal with problems caused by budgets under the predicted cost than ones that are over.

5.8 MANAGING CHANGE

Change management provides a set of theories and tools that extend beyond project management, and are essential for delivering the sustained change that many projects require. There are many sources of change (Table 5.7). There will certainly be changes during the implementation phase of a project, and some project activities are in themselves planned to cause a change. These are often difficult to manage, but planning, monitoring, and control will aid you in administering these aspects effectively.

Changes in the immediate environment of a project affect its activities or objectives. In some cases external changes can be predicted, and there will be some guidance on what actions to take. If the change is unanticipated but significant, a project manager should seek the advice of the sponsor before taking any action that might alter the direction of the project.

It is also important to keep in mind that changes may come suddenly. Some stakeholders cannot give a project the attention it needs until a later date. If you are not receiving change requests, do not assume it is because there are no changes. Instead, realize that the stakeholders may be too busy at this point to care about your project. Often it will take a while for your project to get on their radar, and you must be flexible to their suggestions.

You will encounter two types of changes: changes that have happened, and those that need to happen. Identify and process them promptly to

Table 5.7 Sources of Change

- Overoptimistic time estimations
- Omission of one or more tasks
- Lack or loss of resources
- Strategic adjustment of priorities
- Loss of senior management interest and support
- Funding change
- New personnel
- Usage change
- A realized risk
- Added benefits
- Poor planning
- Modified objectives
- Interference due to increases in other workloads
- Decisions not made on time
- Indecision
- Poor teamwork and coordination

minimize their adverse effects and maximize their positive effects. The first response to a change is usually to understand it and evaluate its impact on the project.

A value-added change is one that adds to the return on investment of a project, such as an additional feature or a scope change. This involves payback analysis and the determination of costs to make informed decisions.

Gold plating, on the other hand, is the addition of features that are outside the scope of the project, are not requested, and do not add value. Gold plating typically happens when well-meaning team members think of an idea that becomes part of the project; this often occurs suddenly, without documentation or wider agreement. In other words, project change management processes are bypassed. Although they might be good ideas, they often add unexpected costs and risks to a project. An example of gold plating would be providing additional reports, information, or features not originally part of the scope of the project. These types of changes should be monitored and controlled, so they do not add to the cost of the project.

Change control is necessary to protect the project from the effects of scope creep. If the project team mismanages scope changes, the project may become considerably over budget or behind schedule. A formal change request form should be used to make changes. Templates for change request and change log forms can be found in Appendix E. The project manager should develop a change control process that is used throughout the project (Table 5.8).

Several outcomes are possible after a change request (Table 5.9). The further along the project, the more detrimental the effect of changes: the

Table 5.8 Change Control Process Steps

- All changes must be submitted to the project manager on a change request form.
- Changes are logged using a spreadsheet.
- The team assesses the impact of the change on schedule, budget, and specifications.
- The impact is discussed with the requestor. Often the change request is withdrawn when the effect is known.
- The proposed change is discussed with the sponsor and the users.
- The change is approved or disapproved, and the requestor is informed of the decision.
- Stakeholders are notified of the change if it occurs.
- The change is incorporated into the project plan and deliverables.

Table 5.9 Possible Change Request Outcomes

- Can be accommodated within the project's resources and schedule
- Can be accommodated but will necessitate an extension of the schedule
- Can be accommodated within the schedule, but additional resources will be required
- Can be accommodated but more resources and time will be required
- Cannot be accommodated without a considerable change to the project

more work already done, the more work that has to be undone and redone. Additionally, the more complex the project, the greater the number of required changes in the original project plan. Such changes are a chief cause of cost and schedule overruns, low morale, and poor relationships between stakeholders and users. Each change has a ripple effect. In response to an emerging problem, elements of the project must be modified, but like an uncontrolled chain reaction these then require changes to other elements that impact still others. Rarely does a change occur in isolation.

You may have to renegotiate an extended deadline, a higher budget, a reduced scope, or some combination of these. When renegotiating, remember that any decrease in the schedule that keeps scope constant will increase cost. Likewise, a reduction in cost with the scope constant will increase the time. You and your project sponsor will have to decide which factors are the most critical, and adjust the others accordingly.

If all else fails, rebaselining may be necessary. Rebaselining, or adopting a new project plan, is a last resort when project work is not going according to schedule. Exhaust all possible strategies and approaches to get back on track before you attempt to change the plan itself.

Project management is about ensuring delivery, not about heroics against unassailable odds. Know when to decline changes and how to say "no," which is discussed in Chapter 6. Just because someone thinks he or she needs a change, it does not mean that it is needed or justified.

CHAPTER 6

Communication and Documentation

> When the trust account is high, communication is easy, instant, and effective.
>
> **Stephen R. Covey**

> Much unhappiness has come into the world because of bewilderment and things left unsaid.
>
> **Fyodor Dostoyevsky**

> The single biggest problem in communication is the illusion that it has taken place.
>
> **George Bernard Shaw**

6.1 WRITING THE CHARTER

The authority to begin a project is granted in a variety of ways, depending on the type of project. It may be an internal document signed by the sponsor and project manager, or an elaborate contract with an external client. Some organizations refer to this formal authority to proceed as a project charter. It is also known as a proposal, project datasheet, project specification, or project definition document. Although the phrase "project charter" will be used in this book, the principles outlined apply to any project definition document, whatever it may be called.

Project charters recognize the existence of the project and give the project manager the authority to spend resources on project activities. The charter includes the business need for undertaking the project and, at a high level, the results to be delivered. It consists of preliminary output descriptions that will be refined as the project progresses. It also describes the links between the project's goals and the broader objectives of the organization.

A project charter is a living document that evolves throughout the project. Maintaining an unambiguous, easily accessed description of the project that is approved by your sponsor and other influencers is a powerful tool which you can use to keep a project under control. A well-written charter forms the basis for detailed scoping, planning, and controlling.

Project Management for Information Professionals
ISBN 978-0-08-100127-1
125

Before writing the charter, ask yourself a series of questions to generate thoughts about the project (Table 6.1). The project charter should contain several elements (Table 6.2). The project name is a given, as well as its purpose. This can be a mission statement, a one-line summary of what the project is supposed to achieve, or a more thorough description of its business objectives.

The charter should include the official name, the sponsor, and the project manager. It should contain the project's purpose, business case, milestones, key deliverables, and a summary of costs. If resources, staff, and vendors are known at the launch of the project, list them as well. A description of the project's risks, assumptions, and constraints should be incorporated. Project approval requirements and acceptance criteria should be added too.

Table 6.1 Project Charter Questions

- Who is issuing the project charter?
- Who has driven the initiative to start the project?
- What is the project's purpose? What problem is it addressing?
- What benefits are expected from the project? Over what period are they anticipated?
- Who will benefit from this project? Who are the stakeholders?
- Who is the project manager? What is the project manager's authority level? For decisions beyond his or her authority, to whom does the project manager report to?
- Does the charter contain a statement of the mission and objectives of the organization?
- Does it identify the business needs that the project will address?
- Does it specify how the project aligns with the organization's mission?
- Does the charter contain deliverables?
- Has the financial analysis been completed for the life cycle of the project?
- Does the charter provide guidance as to how the project will be performed?
- What are the conditions under which the project will take place?
- Does the charter state what resources will be involved?
- Does it outline the organization's responsibilities regarding resources and decisions?
- Does it include statements of what constitutes success?
- Does it provide explanations of how success will be measured?
- Are there any specific scope inclusions or exclusions?
- How long may the project take? What are the important dates?
- What investments will be necessary, and over what period?
- What assumptions were made when identifying timescales, budgets, or benefits?
- What may cause the project to fail? How will risks be mitigated?

Table 6.2 Project Charter Components

- Name
- Purpose of the project
- Description
- Business need
- Scope statement
- Summary milestone schedule
- Summary budget
- Requirements
- Objectives
- Deliverables
- Completion date
- Budget
- Success factors
- Success measures
- Assumptions
- Risks
- Constraints
- Links to strategic objectives and other projects
- Identification of stakeholders, sponsors, and other interested parties
- Identification of the project manager, including role, responsibility, and level of authority

The project manager must be named in the charter, as well as his or her responsibilities and extent of authority. Also integrated is a formal statement of the sponsor's support. The charter begins the chain of commitment by putting in writing the sponsor's support for the project and its manager. The charter is a proclamation that management has given the project manager its backing. Organizations use it to announce and authorize the start of internal projects. All the main stakeholders must approve the project charter as a token of their agreement on the project definition. This announcement is like a power of attorney, stating that the project manager is authorized to perform specific tasks under the authority of the sponsor.

The purpose of the charter is to describe the project to stakeholders and establish the project manager's authority to gather and make use of resources. It includes a variety of information—whatever is necessary to give the reader an overview of the project. For example, it describes the project objectives, scope, stakeholders, estimated budget and schedule, risks, assumptions, constraints, and resources. Often the charter contains sections similar to the project plan; indeed, sometimes it is used as the project plan. More commonly, it is brief, several pages at most, and provides an overview of a more comprehensive project plan.

6.2 ESTABLISHING THE COMMUNICATION PLAN

The advantage of creating and managing communications is that you can control the information flow and use the plan to support the project and everyone involved in it. A communication strategy takes into account both internal and external communications. Internal communications are those within the project team, while external communications are those between the project and its stakeholders. A template for a communications plan can be found in Appendix E.

How will the project manager and team communicate their work to people beyond the project team? Questions regarding the communication plan can help determine these answers (Table 6.3). The external communication plan is a vital part of the process, and involves managing the information flow to stakeholders. Ideally, stakeholders should be kept informed about the project throughout the process so they do not receive any unexpected surprises. Communication occurs throughout the project life cycle through initiation, planning, monitoring, and closure (Table 6.4). Communication methods vary according to type and audience (Table 6.5). For example, team members will receive communication about the project more frequently and more granularly than will sponsors.

Table 6.3 Communication Plan Questions

- What are the requirements for reporting and meetings imposed by project documents?
- What are the policies and procedures regarding status reporting?
- What are the external communication requirements?
- How will the information needs of each stakeholder be satisfied?
- What formal reports will be produced to satisfy stakeholder requirements?
- What types of reports will be produced?
- What project meetings will occur?
- How will you share information among team members?
- Who is responsible for generating and distributing the various types of communications?
- What are the events, milestones, and deliverable dates that will initiate communication?
- How will you handle *ad hoc* inquiries the project is likely to encounter?
- Have you developed a project information database and assigned responsibilities for its maintenance?
- Are there ways to evaluate the effectiveness of the communication plan?
- How will you update or change the communication plan, if needed?
- What is the approval process required for communications?
- Has the project team reviewed the communication plan?

Table 6.4 Communication through the Life-Cycle

Phase	Messages	Audience
Initiation	• Benefits: Why are we doing this? • Success criteria: How will we know we have done a good job? • Organization structure: How will we manage this project?	• Project manager • Sponsor • Users
Planning	• Commitment: What is the plan we have agreed to do? • Team: Who is doing the work?	• Project manager • Project team • Other staff affected by the project • Sponsor • Users • Vendors/third parties
Monitoring	• Deliverables: What tasks are we doing and who is doing them? • Progress: How are we doing regarding the schedule and the budget? • Control: How are we measuring and controlling risks, issues, and quality? • Approval: Should we be moving to the next delivery phase?	• Project manager • Project team • Other staff affected by the project • Sponsor • Users • Vendors/third parties
Closure	• Evaluation: How did we perform against our success criteria? • Status: Can we confirm that the project is closed? • Handover: Who are we handing the project over to and have they accepted the project's outputs? • Team: What is the team going to work on next?	• Project manager • Project team • Other staff affected by the project • Sponsor • Users • Vendors/third parties • Wider audience

The best communication methods use as few words as possible to convey their meaning. Tailor the message for the particular audience to give them what they need. Good communication methods use media that make the audience most likely to look at the communication, and explicate what actions the audience need to take, if any. The communication vehicle should also blend into the organizational culture, so that reading about the

Table 6.5 Project Communications Overview

What activity?	Who is involved?	Why should we do this?	When should it happen?
Project kick-off	Project manager, team, stakeholders, and sponsor	To develop relationships and build trust	At or near project start date
Status reports	Stakeholders and team	To update stakeholders on project progress	Regularly scheduled weekly or monthly
Team communications	Team	To build and review tasks, assignments, and action items	Regularly scheduled weekly or monthly
Sponsor communication	Sponsor and project manager	To decide on critical issues and scope changes	Monthly and as needed
Postproject review	Project manager, team, stakeholders, and sponsor	To review accomplishments and identify needed improvements	End of project or major phase

project is embedded into the audience's workflow. For example, if emails are the standard communication tool in your organization, use email as a way to transmit information about your project.

It is helpful to create a stakeholder register that clarifies everyone's roles. You can categorize stakeholders based on their communication needs to determine their power, impact, interest, and influence. Power represents executive management roles. Impact differs from power. With many projects you might only have indirect access to senior executives; Instead, you will have to work with someone whose job it is to update them. This person may lack power, but will impact your project and may have great control over it. Lastly are your stakeholders, who have an influence on your project; they will guide it. Different stakeholders will have various levels of attentiveness to your project, so you want to categorize them based on their interest levels. Using these categorized stakeholders, prioritize them based on their relationship to the project. The stakeholder matrix described in Chapter 3 (Figure 3.1) can be used to prioritize communication based on stakeholders' power and interest.

Project communication management includes identifying stakeholders, planning communications, distributing information, managing stakeholder expectations, and reporting performance. The communication plan describes the expectations and needs for the project. It specifies what information will be exchanged, when and how it will be communicated, and who will impart it and to whom.

The flow of data needs to be designed to ensure that information reaches the people who need it. The format in which data is recorded, stored, and retrieved determines how it can be used and by whom. The methods used to collect and distribute information will also influence how it is understood and used.

The time and energy that are put into external communications will depend on the nature of the project. In larger projects, the project team may have a working party whose primary consideration is the external communication process. A strategy to ensure that all aspects of external communications are considered involves identifying the purpose of the communication strategy, who handles its implementation, and who will be working on the project. You will also need to determine what and when you will communicate, and to whom.

To develop an external communications strategy, you will need to use as many different forms of communication as possible, such as meetings, presentations, workshops, press releases, and emails. You will also need to repeat your message many times over the period of the project.

You may rely on a variety of push and pull communication methods. For example, the project may have a portal where all project documents are stored and accessible to anyone related to the project. The team also pushes project communication to stakeholders through emails and meetings. Offering the data in multiple formats allows all stakeholders to access the information they need in the format they prefer.

The basis of a good communications strategy starts with the development of a targeted communication plan. This plan should be able to satisfy the specific informational needs of those involved throughout the life cycle of the project. For instance, a steering committee may only need to be communicated with on a monthly basis, whereas the project team may require weekly status meetings.

An effective communication strategy puts in place a process for gaining commitment from the stakeholder community at large. Part of this process is to establish effective two-way communication and the need for different messages over time. During the project life cycle, your needs for communication may vary. For instance, the early stages of your project will require a lot of communication to ensure that stakeholders know what is going to happen, who will be involved, and why your project has been initiated. Once the project gets under way, the need for communication may lessen to the point of simply providing periodic updates on key milestones, accomplishments, or issues.

Avoid under- or overcommunicating. Regular project communiqués explain to stakeholders what is happening in ways that engage them without wasting their time. Stakeholders are displeased with communication vehicles that are too brief and tend to generate more questions than answers. Instead, they want enough information to answer their questions, but not so much as to inundate them with data.

A good communications plan sets realistic expectations as well as becoming a platform for issue resolution and decision-making. It is crucial for dealing with stakeholders, so they are confident in your role as project manager and their commitments can be maintained.

6.3 CREATING PROJECT DOCUMENTATION

In an influential and well-known book on software engineering projects, *The Mythical Man-Month*, Frederick P. Brooks Jr. (1995) writes:

> To the new manager, fresh from operating as a craftsman himself, [documentation] seem an unmitigated nuisance, an unnecessary distraction, and a white tide that threatens to engulf him. And indeed, most of them are exactly that. Bit by bit, however, he comes to realize that a certain small set of these documents embodies and expresses much of his managerial work. The preparation of each one serves as a major occasion for focusing thought and crystallizing discussions that otherwise would wander endlessly. Its maintenance becomes his surveillance and warning mechanism. The document itself serves as a check list, a status control, and a data base [sic] for his reporting (p. 108).

As Brooks so keenly states, documentation is an area of project work that is frequently overlooked to ensure that tasks are completed on time, yet it serves many purposes (Table 6.6).

Documentation is often seen as bureaucratic and tedious. It is associated with busywork that takes away from real work. This perception will never be eradicated, but it can be minimized. In practice, a balance should exist between written reporting, conversations, and group discussions that elaborate on matters raised in written reports wherever necessary.

Table 6.6 Purpose of Documentation

- Reference for future changes in deliverables
- Records for estimating time and cost on projects and tasks
- Training resource for future project managers
- Source for training and development of the team
- Resource to identify areas where projects should be managed better
- Input for performance evaluation for the functional managers of the team members

Focus the team on documentation by directing efforts to its production early in the project process. Doing so is one of the best ways to ensure it will be delivered. This prevents procrastination on documentation until the last two or three months before the close of the project, and requires the team to include documentation production from the start of the project work.

Whenever you ask people to do something that seems to be additional work, such as regularly filling out data input forms, you must help them understand why you are asking them to do this and how it will make their lives easier. If you fail to explain the reasoning behind the work, team members are likely to resist the process or ignore it.

Consider creating a WBS-based spreadsheet to track labor hours spent, current statuses, forecasted values, problems, or reestimates of duration and cost. You can also provide copies of the project schedule that team members can fill in as appropriate to provide information on project statuses. There are many possibilities to enable your team members to give you information. Whatever you choose, take the time and effort to make documentation easier for them and yourself.

The project manager should ensure that a project repository has been established and all the relevant documentation generated in every step of the project has been filed in it. The repository can be as simple as a binder or as complex as a document management system. Contents should include all materials that represent the bulk of the project (Table 6.7). These documents will be essential when compiling your project archives once the project closes, which is explained further in Chapter 7.

Documentation can also come from regular progress evaluations. Team-generated reports record information you collect in your team meetings. If your organization can store and retrieve project data, such as labor hours or material costs, you should download this data periodically and keep the documents in your project file.

Table 6.7 Project Repository Contents

- Project charter
- Kickoff meeting documentation
- Project plan
  - Work breakdown structure
  - Project schedule
  - Project budget
  - Resource plan
  - Communication plan
  - Change control plan
  - Risk plan
- Status reports
- Change requests and approvals
- Meeting minutes
- Lessons learned
- Closeout checklist

6.4 REPORTING PROJECT PERFORMANCE

Communication about project performance is important, because if people lack understanding about what is expected of them, they will fail to deliver against project tasks. Those indirectly involved with a project but with a stake in seeing it completed need to be communicated with in a way that engages them without wasting their time. Long reports, detailed analysis, and extended discussions are unnecessary.

Effective communication is essential in understanding issues that arise as the project unfolds, and in maintaining progress. Reporting and review systems provide a means of communication, but may be insufficient in meeting all the needs of those working on the project.

For regular reports, stakeholders want to know the highlights. Reports should be short, preferably no longer than a page of bullet points that keep stakeholders focused on critical issues. Activities in the report transmit what you have been doing, what has been completed, and what has started. You should also state if a task has been delayed. Planned activities should be discussed. What is due to happen next, according to the plan? If there has been a problem, what needs to be done to resolve it? Problems are the area on which stakeholders are most likely to concentrate, and where you as a project manager can draw on their experience and influence. Finally, review the budget. What has been spent and how much is left?

Management must be kept appraised of the status, progress, and performance of ongoing and upcoming projects. Problems affecting schedules, budgets, and quality, as well as their expected impacts and recommended actions, should be reported promptly.

Executive stakeholders will need to be managed closely. Often your project will be sponsored by one of the organization's executives, who will have performance expectations. He or she will also have semantics that differ from project management lingo, which tends to be technical and detail-oriented.

Executive stakeholders care about a surprisingly minimal amount of the work a project team is doing. They want to know if the team is on track; they expect the project manager to care about and manage the details. If you continually give them the impression that the project is out of control, you lose credibility.

Communicating with your executives is a dual challenge. Not only do you need to make sure you are managing communications well, you also need to use the same terms that the executive accepts. The sponsor for your project could have a portfolio of projects. He or she will have invested a lot of political capital into the portfolio, so the sponsor will be interested in, but not solely focused on, details. Sponsors will be concerned with successful delivery, which makes their motivations different from yours as a project manager. The project manager is focused on delivering the project on time and on budget.

When you talk to sponsors, use the language of quality and delivery. If they ask you about a project, list the recent accomplishments and let them know if the project is on schedule. Be concise. An elevator pitch, or a 30-second summary, should be enough of an update about the project. Instead of delving into the minutiae of the WBS, speak about how the project will deliver results. Usually sponsors dislike hearing about challenges unless there are recommendations for fixes, so never give your sponsor a catalog of issues that you are currently resolving. It will be perceived as you not doing the job of project management.

The final aspect to keep in mind when you are talking to a sponsor is to have a big picture of where your project fits into his or her overall portfolio. Your sponsor will have challenges beyond just your project, and will appreciate that you can communicate how your project fits into the organization as a whole.

6.5 COMMUNICATING WITH THE TEAM

If the project involves interdisciplinary or interorganizational work, the value of productive interaction cannot be overestimated. When people have various backgrounds, it is difficult to establish enough trust and confidence in each other to work effectively. Although communication can reveal differences, opportunities exist to identify similarities and concerns. Support for the aims of a project provide the chance to identify a common ground in values. If people develop enthusiasm to achieve goals, it is easier to work together.

Many project managers who have technical backgrounds find it difficult to deal with people effectively. They are task-oriented rather than people-oriented, and some may dislike this aspect of the job. Some people tend to focus on the technical rather than the human side of the job not because the work is more crucial, but because it is easier to do. Human interactions are complicated, but they matter more than any other aspect of project work. Although project management includes techniques that are straightforward, most of the work requires soft skills. In fact, people skills often surpass technical skills in getting projects completed successfully. Project managers must manage and motivate their teams to deliver all that is required for the project. Project management methodologies alone are unable to achieve this. A project manager, above all else, is a people manager.

Communicating, negotiating, leading, coaching, and working with people can consume a lifetime of study. Proficiency with people skills is vital to project management. Project managers must be able to seek advice and counsel from their teams, yet also push back when the team and stakeholders veer off course. They must be able to keep their momentum going forward. This requires an extraordinary amount of diplomacy and empathy. The project manager must get people to perform outside of their regular duties without the formal authority to do so. Trust in the team must be present, or the project may have below-par results. Interpersonal relationships are essential elements to the success of any project. People are the most valuable asset for projects, and knowing how to manage them is the difference between a spectacular project and a failure.

The position of the project manager is privileged, in that he or she has access to every aspect of the project. In many ways it is a lonely role. Although the group can discuss issues, people may be unprepared to share concerns with the project manager. He or she should be trusted with confidential matters. Often project managers may be drawn into situations

Table 6.8 Motivational Factors

- Fear: Inactivity may bring about unwanted results, attention, or punishments.
- Ambition: Personal achievement can motivate people to excel if they believe their current actions will help them reach future goals.
- Recognition: Sometimes a public recognition, commendation, or mention of their hard work is enough to motivate people
- Rewards: Financial gain, vacation days, or other rewards can motivate people to action.
- Avoidance: Inaction may bring about results that the person wants to avoid.
- Peer pressure: When a project team is working together, it is harder for individuals to withdraw from the project.
- Expectations: When a person is assigned activities to complete by someone he or she admires and respects, the person will work harder to meet expectations.

in which one group is discussing another, and if managers seem to be taking sides it will be difficult to maintain a trusted position. Most project managers, even experienced ones, need support from someone who has a wider perspective. It can be helpful to have a mentor with whom to discuss issues in confidence.

A project manager empowers others. His or her job is to get the work completed, to get scarce resources, and to buffer teams from distractions that can disrupt the work. The project manager can employ several motivational factors to support the team (Table 6.8).

One of the primary concerns of a project manager is to ensure that everyone who needs information receives the right data when they require it. This can be planned using each activity on the schedule. Each person or team needs to know when they can start work and whether anything has happened in the previous period that will affect the next period. This knowledge involves information from formal written plans and face-to-face meetings at critical handover points.

Effective teams have a shared sense of purpose, which is reflected in their communication. Team members talk openly, honestly, and respectfully with each other. Communicating takes trust, but it also builds confidence. The project charter documents this for teams. Sometimes the team puts together its vision statement along with a list of team values. The collaborative effort to record a particular team vision and values builds cohesiveness and enhances the shared sense of purpose.

The channels of communication should include everyone who is involved in a project. The members of the project team have to communicate with anyone completing related activities. People outside the team should be kept informed and have opportunities for their voices to be heard, including stakeholders and sponsors. Communication involves giving and receiving. If we miscommunicate with each other, we may find ourselves working at cross-purposes. We lose the opportunity to influence and be influenced by others' ideas.

Communication may be formal or informal, depending on the size of the project, the people involved, and their work methods, but it must happen if the project is to succeed. Team members can become immersed in their activities and fail to seek or listen to feedback from anyone outside the team. A communications strategy will consider how to provide mechanisms through which the essential two-way communication can take place.

Communication can be improved by paying attention to the needs of other people, listening actively, and checking that messages have been understood. Project managers should also pay attention to the feedback they hear, give feedback, and be able to choose the time and place to have difficult or confidential conversations.

One area of communication that is often overlooked is the importance of providing the right information to team members. Essential information for team members that is valid over the entire project life cycle includes project context, goals, team members' roles and responsibilities, project schedule, and chain of command and reporting relationships.

Do what you say and say what you mean. Admit when you are wrong. Enlist the opinions and ideas of others in decisions that affect them. By doing these things, you will earn the trust of your team. When a time comes where you must ask them to do something that they do not wish to do, their trust in you will make your leadership possible.

6.6 HANDLING PROBLEMS

Communication is necessary to link the stages of a project and facilitate progress within each stage. It is central to the management of a project. Poor communication can threaten the likelihood of completing the project successfully.

Conflicts occur in all phases of the project life cycle and at any level—between functional groups, and among the stakeholders. Project

Table 6.9 Conflict Causes and Solutions

Causes	Solutions
Overlapping responsibilities	• Clear activity definition • Unambiguous delegation
Differing cultures or perspectives	• Effectual team management • Conducting kick-off meeting • Avoiding unnecessary interactions
Misunderstandings	• Thorough communications planning • Effective communications control
Lack of trust	• Periodic face-to-face meetings • Coaching and mentoring • Building influence without authority

managers often assume the role of conflict manager, and may be required to respond to a range of issues with several solutions (Table 6.9).

The ability to handle conflict requires an understanding of why conflicts occur, the sources of conflict, and the specific needs of the stakeholders involved. In many cases, conflict begins with poorly defined objectives and unclear roles and responsibilities.

When dealing with conflict, never get upset. Try to remain calm and professional. Do not mistake conflicts about a project as being a personal attack or a judgment about the quality of your work or your authority. When determining the cause of conflict and its resolution, use examples from the project to make your point. Empathize and show concern with the problem, recognize the frustration it causes, and assure everyone that you want to find a solution. Look for the reasons behind requests and actions. Trying to understand people's motivations helps you respond appropriately to team members, executives, and stakeholders; and this, in turn, increases people's motivation and buy-in. The more clearly you describe your intended results, the more easily people can recognize the benefits associated with your project. The better you define your work, the more often people will ask insightful questions and believe that they can perform the work successfully. Lucidity leads to increased personal motivation and reduced chances of mistakes.

The role of the project manager and the team in problem-solving includes identifying problems and determining the various options for resolution (Table 6.10). Problem-solving is crucial to developing and working on a project. The ability to provide problem-solving in difficult

Table 6.10 Conflict Resolution Methods

Method	Description
Confronting	Approaching an issue point-blank. The project manager recognizes that disagreement among team members is a source of positive creative energy. Confronting is designed to maintain trust and respect within teams while working through conflicts. A win—win outcome.
Compromising	Utilizing negotiation to reach a resolution. Each side accepts less than it wishes, with the consolation that it got as much as the other side. Compromise satisfies no one, and the disappointment can cause resentment. A neutral outcome.
Withdrawal	Ignoring a conflict in hopes that it will disappear. This approach delays the inevitable conflict and increases the pressure. A lose—lose outcome.
Smoothing	This strategy focuses on the positive relationships and de-emphasizes areas of conflict. It prioritizes relationships over resolving disagreements, which is a short-term solution. A lose—lose outcome.
Forcing	Utilizing power to make a decision. There may be little commitment to the decision by those upon whom it was forced upon. This method threatens the positive relationships required in high-performance teams. A win-lose outcome.

situations involves creativity and can be challenging. First, the project manager must define the problem in words that everyone can understand. The team utilizes ingenuity to develop solutions and make decisions based on input from other participants. The decision-making process involves problem analysis, feedback solicitation, and choosing the best alternative.

For most problems, confronting the issue and working on solutions is the best approach to resolving issues in such a way that everyone wins. Negotiating may be one way to resolve conflicts, and there are several techniques to utilize (Table 6.11). The ability to negotiate resolutions to conflicts effectively can determine the success of your project. The process of obtaining support from participants is necessary if you need to have the involvement of your team. Team members tend to work more diligently toward goals when they have been involved in the development process and have given their input.

After the options have been determined, the project manager must make a decision to choose the best alternative. There are several

Table 6.11 Negotiation Techniques

Preparing

- Clarify what you are negotiating.
- Write down your ideal settlement.
- Identify the worst you will agree to accept.
- Name the strengths and weaknesses of your case.
- Determine the other party's knowledge of your needs.
- Recognize the other party's likely objections.
- Specify the issues that the other party will raise.
- Spot the strengths and weaknesses of their argument.
- Verify the benefits you can offer the other party.
- Check how other party behaved in other negotiations.

Bargaining

- Open by asking for more than you expect to get.
- Let the other party talk and listen actively.
- Ask questions to determine the other party's position.
- Focus on interests, not positions.
- Insist on objective, fact-based criteria for discussion, analysis, and decisions.
- Focus on problem-solving, not arguing about the project.
- Do not accept the first offer.
- Never suggest more than you have the power to give.
- Work together to brainstorm and explore options for mutual gain.
- Consider all implications before accepting a concession.
- Remain objective, assertive, and calm.

Concluding

- Summarize your agreement.
- Agree on what issues should be referred to the sponsor, if any.
- Clarify and confirm the benefits to the other party.

decision-making methods to choose from (Table 6.12). The project manager should solicit feedback from team members and encourage their buy-in so that everyone takes part in the process.

Some problems become uncontrollable because they must be passed up several layers of authority before they can be resolved. You must set up a procedure for communication with higher management, called an escalation procedure, when a project begins to exceed cost or schedule. The escalation procedure will determine which level of management to contact, depending on the degree of variance from the plan.

If a problem is personal or sensitive, it is best to deal with it one-on-one in private. As you clear roadblocks, answer questions, and check in with

Table 6.12 Decision Making Methods

Method	Description	Speed	Commitment
Consultative	Members are encouraged to discuss ideas and opinions; The decision-maker decides	Fast	High
Consensus	Everyone's concerns and interests are addressed, and members agree on the decision	Slowest	Highest
Authoritative	The group leader chooses the result	Fastest	Lowest
Voting	Everyone votes and the majority wins	Fast	Low

various people, remember that the effort you put into these tasks is important. As long as you can connect those discussions back to positive trends in the project or the prevention of negative ones, they are essential to moving the project forward.

One of the thorniest people issues faced by project managers is conflict among team members. Bringing individuals together from different parts of an organization to complete a mission always presents opportunities for conflict. Ironically, one of the essential characteristics of a well-structured team—diversity of thinking, backgrounds, and skills—is itself a potential source of conflict.

The project manager must encourage members to listen to each other, be willing to understand different viewpoints, and question each other's assumptions. He or she must prevent conflict from becoming personal or being repressed, where resentment simmers.

When certain issues evolve in projects, sometimes you have to say "no." This is difficult for project managers because organizations disparage the word—project managers are rewarded for their ability to get things done. However, sometimes declining a request is the correct answer. Project managers face two choices: you can turn down the demand, or you can accept the appeal and own the outcome. You will be responsible for the failed project if you say "yes" when you should not. This is more dangerous than being seen as a negative person.

Every project manager should be able to decline requests correctly. One way to do so is to give a decisive "no" that is enclosed between good news and empathy. It shows that you have listened to the stakeholder's concerns, sympathize with him or her, but must refuse nevertheless. Another option is to say "Yes, but," and list your reservations. Stakeholders are less likely to feel they are being turned down and more apt to listen to the reasons why you cannot implement their requests. You can also ask them to choose what they would rather have: the realization of their request or the forfeiture of other project aspects. Asking them to choose is an effective way to reframe situations where you are facing unrealistic expectations.

6.7 CONDUCTING MEETINGS

Meetings punctuate projects. They are the least-favorite activity of action-oriented people but, when done well, are often the best way to communicate information. Meetings also provide forums within which ideas can be shared and decisions made. Progress depends on those decisions. Thus, if your project must have meetings, get the most out of them.

Meetings have many purposes (Table 6.13). They share the team's information about the project's progress so that status reports can be prepared, any issues dealt with, and everybody knows what has to be done next. They solve problems through brainstorming; generate ideas, options, and alternatives; and require decision-making skills. Participants select a course of action, and gain support and commitment from team members. Planning, evaluation, monitoring, feedback, and forecasting are also conducted in meetings.

Large conference-style meetings work when you are launching a project, but many people find them an ineffective use of their time. Instead, a smaller, more efficient forum is an action or work group meeting. Three

Table 6.13 Meeting Purposes

- Reviewing action items from the previous meeting
- Updating work progress
- Discussing existing problems and giving guidance
- Anticipating potential difficulties
- Forecasting the completion of current tasks
- Reviewing upcoming tasks
- Assessing other commitments and priorities
- Evaluating performance
- Assessing risks
- Recognizing team members' achievements
- Identifying training needs and how to satisfy them
- Resolving interpersonal problems

to five people seems to be a good number for participants to collaborate effectively. Their meeting is designed to solve a singular, discrete problem, such as why a program keeps crashing or why an employee is under-performing. The meeting has one set of objectives: to solve the problem put forth in the group.

It is wise to meet with only some members of the team if the agenda of a meeting is geared toward just those individuals. Project managers may feel the need to involve the entire team in every discussion related to the project, but this is often unnecessary. Sometimes the objectives of a meeting are geared to a few individuals. These meetings should be separate and in addition to the regularly scheduled team meetings.

Making the most of meetings involves keeping a regular schedule as much as possible. If people know that project team meetings take place at a particular time, they can plan their other responsibilities around those hours. A regular schedule saves meeting organizers the time-consuming task of finding a time on which everyone can agree.

Meetings have to be necessary. If you can accomplish your goal without calling a meeting, do so. Every meeting should have its objectives clarified. Each attendee should be able to answer the question, "Why am I here?" If the purpose is to make a decision, be sure that everyone understands this in advance and has the time and materials needed to prepare.

The right people should be involved. Only invite those who have something to contribute, whose participation is necessary, or who can learn from the discussion. Invite those who are essential to the agenda, and no one else. The more people in your meeting, the more difficult it will be to stay on the subject and get anything done. Additionally, limit the duration of the meetings. If your meetings run for too long, you will not achieve results.

Stand-up meetings are those in which attendees stand to give a brief update on what they are doing. Depending on the type of project you are performing, you might want to conduct these meetings daily or every other day. They are short, and allow information to be exchanged quickly.

Provide an agenda beforehand so that each attendee can prepare for the discussions scheduled to take place. This will save time during meetings as well as avoid the necessity of additional meetings due to unprepared participants. If a topic appears to be too large to resolve within the allocated time, particularly if the entire group is unnecessary for its resolution, develop an action item and handle it outside the meeting. A template to create meeting agendas may be found in Appendix E.

Always survey participants in advance. You will be better prepared for a meeting if you know what key participants think about important items on the agenda. What you learn may suggest an alteration in the agenda.

In meetings, let others talk first to hear all sides, and then offer your input. Do not be afraid to ask questions. Try to go with the majority, but make your case if you disagree.

Building decisions through consensus often produces superior results because the project manager leverages the knowledge and skills of the team. You reach an agreement when participants concur that the decision process was reasonable, their viewpoints were considered, and they support the decision.

To build consensus, encourage people to use active listening skills. Ensure a balance of power, and prevent the most vocal participant from dominating the conversation. Embrace conflict as a sign of creative thinking, and seek alternative solutions. Find ways to integrate multiple viewpoints. Ensuring participation and decisions that everyone will support is the key to consensus.

For progress meetings, the project manager should review the delivery highlights during the previous period to identify the steps started or completed, and the highlights during the next period. Progress meetings rely on a participative management style holding that involvement leads to ownership, which results in greater commitment and accountability.

Reviewing timescales allows users to scrutinize progress and identify differences against the plan. Assessing budgets identifies variances against the cost plan and clarifies the reasons for those differences so that corrective actions can be considered. Examine quality, risks, issues, actions, and decisions.

End with confirmation and an action plan with clear steps and owners. Phrase activities using active language, starting with an outcome-oriented verb. For example, "create metadata crosswalk," "set up a bibliographic workshop," or "obtain project sign-off." Announce the action item captured, to whom it belongs, and the target resolution date. When a meeting ends, all that matters is what happens next. Never let people leave a room without the next steps identified. During the next meeting, review the previous action steps and follow up on the assigned tasks.

6.8 GENERATING STATUS REPORTS

Status reports provide a communication vehicle to summarize the overall status of each project. They show progress, as well as acting as a vehicle to bring the core issues of the project to the forefront. A mistake is to include everything about the project that anyone might want to know in a status report; instead of informing everyone, such reports may be overwhelming. When developing the report content, keep it practical and brief. A template can be found in Appendix E.

The frequency, content, and format of status reports vary from organization to organization, and yet all are designed to make sure everyone involved understands where the project is at any given point in time.

Organizations use two types of status report. One type summarizes the entire project to date. The project manager issues these monthly. The most common status report, though, is the weekly report, which briefly describes progress since the last report. Team members usually write the reports and send them to the project manager, who then summarizes them and distributes the document back to the team and interested stakeholders.

The first step in creating your status reports is to evaluate the audience. In general, the fewer people who are affected by the project, the less detail they will want in the report. Typically, a team member creates status reports and distributes them to many readers. The information is gathered in a standard format in a predetermined timeframe, and reviewed with the project team prior to issue to other stakeholders. There should be no surprises when the status report is given to anyone who has a need to know.

Additionally, evaluate the audience's technical level. People with a background in the project area will want to have some technical data in the status report. It is okay to use jargon with this group. People without the technical background will need the status expressed in lay terms.

Status reporting describes where the project stands since the last status report. It should include a status summary of the project, showing if it is off track, on track but will soon be off track, or on track. Accomplishments in the reporting period should include the milestones achieved, milestones planned but unachieved, deliverables completed, and work packages planned but incomplete.

The report should describe the status of key tasks, particularly those on the critical path. Tasks that have high levels of risk should be given special attention, as should those being performed by outside vendors, over which the project manager may have limited control.

Also included is a summary of issues regarding risks, changes, issues, and action items. List the accomplishments planned for the next period, such as milestones to be achieved, deliverables to be completed, and decisions that will need to be taken. The report should specify the nature of any deviations expected in the schedule, cost, performance, or scope.

Define any metrics you will use and decide what data you need to receive about the status of the project. Examples include what has been completed, what has not been completed and why, what is being done about the incomplete work, what problems remain unsolved, and what difficulties are anticipated in the work still to be done.

The simpler and more straightforward a status report, the better. The information conveyed should be organized so that planned versus actual results can be compared easily. Deviations of a significant nature should be explained.

Status reports are stored by date, with each subsequent report stored as an additional file. This lets you maintain a record of methods that work and do not work throughout your project.

CHAPTER 7

Completion and Review

Human beings, who are almost unique in having the ability to learn from the experience of others, are also remarkable for their apparent disinclination to do so.

Douglas Adams

A hard beginning maketh a good ending.

John Heywood

Great is the art of beginning, but greater is the art of ending.

Henry Wadsworth Longfellow

7.1 VERIFYING THE SCOPE

Closing a project involves several activities to review and evaluate its success. To determine how the project performed, consult your objectives and compare them to the completed deliverables. Did the project deliverables satisfy the objectives? If they did, you have accomplished the most important part of the project. If you fell short, record why and what needs to be done to rectify this.

Before a project closes, verify its scope. Testing the scope examines the project's total range of activities to determine the effectiveness of the project. Support documents should be validated by comparing them to the requirements of the project plan.

If you are completing a project with multiple phases, having scope verification throughout the project is a must. When milestones are reached, usually at the end of a project phase, it is an ideal opportunity to verify the scope. You may also consider scope verification based on your approach to stakeholder management. If there are deliverables that an important stakeholder is concerned with, invite him or her to inspect those deliverables often. This confirms that what you are creating is what he or she asked for. If project managers follow this process, errors will be infrequent. This is why is it is important for the project requirements to be accurately defined and agreed upon early in the project. If everyone is in agreement as to what the project is to create, has documented requirements and expectations for

Project Management for Information Professionals
ISBN 978-0-08-100127-1

the project work, and follows the change control system, there will be little variance between what was asked for and what is delivered.

When the project necessitates the production of deliverables, the project manager needs to conduct an audit to verify that all are present. Do this by reviewing your deliverables, comparing them to the deliverables listed in your plan, and making sure that each matches the quality, integrity, and completeness attributes noted in the plan. Incomplete deliverables or those with quality problems must be fixed. Turning over substandard products is often worse than delivering nothing.

A project is complete and successful when all requirements have been met. It is important that the requirements were set thoughtfully and that they are measurable and verifiable to define project completion.

The deliverables that have been accepted through the scope verification and procurement closure processes still need to go through final acceptance by appropriate parties, such as the users or the sponsor. The groups must verify the completion of all activities. A functional audit of the project will indicate that everything is completed and evaluated. Discrepancies must be identified and resolved.

If there are any exceptions noted where your project might be incomplete in one or more requirements, document them and address any deficiencies by extending your project to accommodate additional work if necessary. You can also renegotiate the project scope to be consistent with what you produced, or obtain conditional sign-off and commit to resolution in the future. Even when there are insufficiencies in the project, get a written acknowledgment of what you did deliver.

7.2 MANAGING CLAIMS

During the final phase of the project, stakeholders have the least amount of influence while project managers have the greatest amount. Costs are significantly lower during the closing period because a majority of the project work and spending has already occurred. This is an ideal period to concentrate on the final details of the project.

Good project management requires a benefits realization phase. Benefits are the main drivers of projects. Many project managers focus on generating deliverables while not giving attention to the expected outcomes, or benefits, of the project. These benefits include project quality, timeliness, budget compliance, and the degree of user satisfaction. Although many benefits accrue after a project is complete, it is also smart to measure them at the end of a project to confirm that they outweighed the investment made.

Benefits are difficult to quantify, especially in archives, libraries, and museums. For instance, how can a value be placed on increased user satisfaction or improved morale? User satisfaction means that patron expectations are met. This involves a combination of conformance to requirements and fitness for use. In other words, the project must produce what it said it would, and the products or services created by the project must satisfy real needs. Benefits must be quantified at the outset and measured at the end of the benefits realization phase if an organization is to judge whether it made a worthwhile investment.

Project managers should also carry out a rigorous review of the project. They should check that the team has finished work and completed tasks on time. It is common to find tasks from earlier stages unfinished. They have not impeded progress until now, yet they must be completed.

Project managers should focus on outstanding issues and allocate responsibility for each, with target dates for resolution. When they are satisfied that everything is under control, project managers should confirm the date of the formal closing of the project with their sponsors.

There is often a rush to complete a project in its final stages, which can cause quality issues. Quality should never be sacrificed for an immediate gain in time. Often the final parts of the project are the most evident to stakeholders, so there must be consistent diligence regarding quality implementation.

Throughout the project, confirm clear definitions of what it will look like when it closes. The process of writing and maintaining project acceptance begins with gathering requirements. It is documented during planning, maintained throughout project execution, and applied in the closing phase of the project.

7.3 CLOSING THE PROJECT

When the work is completed, close the project in a controlled manner. This allows the project team to evaluate the project's achievements against its objectives and deliverables. Additionally, hand over the operational elements of a project to whoever will maintain it.

Have a meeting to evaluate the project. You may want to speak first with your team to prepare a wrap-up presentation for stakeholders. A series of meetings may be required to draw conclusions about overall project performance. Any constraints encountered should be considered, and proposals to overcome them in the future noted. The project manager may identify and review new ways of working, bearing in mind what was effective and what should have been done differently.

The project manager may handle reviewing the project team members' performance on the project. When team members work on a project for a lengthy period, their line managers may have lost insight into their performance, making it difficult for them to suggest raises, promotions, or demotions. Throughout the project, the project manager should present reports to team members' managers regarding performance. Be accurate, fair, and professional, and rely on the project documentation you have compiled throughout the project. Staff evaluation also gives the project manager more authority. When team members understand that you will report their performance to their managers, they will be motivated to perform better.

A useful approach to the performance review is the 360° appraisal, in which every person on the project team considers all the other participants in the project, including the project manager. Most often, this evaluation will include direct feedback from subordinates, peers, and supervisors, as well as a self-evaluation. It can also include feedback from external sources, such as vendors or other interested stakeholders. This approach helps the organization's management team find trends and make accurate assessments, and takes some of the review pressure off the project manager.

One of the most useful tools you will use is feedback on yourself as the project manager. Ask your team, sponsor, and stakeholders to be candid with their reactions because it will aid your development as a project manager. Take the feedback graciously, and be honest with yourself about the improvements you need to make to enhance your performance during your next project.

In some projects, closure activities are small projects in themselves, and project managers should plan them as a set of tasks called a punch list. Most of these activities are absent from your original project plan because loose ends and unexpected issues often accompany the waning days of a project. Do a thorough review of the project, because sometimes people cut corners to move on to their next project. Create a list of final items and review it to ensure that everything is completed and the quality of the work is satisfactory. A project completion checklist assumes nothing is overlooked (Table 7.1). Often some nonurgent details are outstanding as the delivery date approaches.

Table 7.1 Project Completion Checklist

- Ensure unfinished activities are completed.
- Have a meeting to evaluate the project.
- Meet with stakeholders and sponsors to approve or sign off on the project.
- Finish accounting procedures such as paying bills and fulfilling contracts.
- Review the project results achieved.
- Go through the handover checklist.
- Confirm and explain action plans for any outstanding issues.
- Agree upon and establish responsibilities for ongoing support.
- Confirm who is responsible for gathering project benefits.
- Transfer documentation to those responsible for maintaining project results.
- Meet with and thank team members for their work.
- Reassign team members.
- Return equipment and any borrowed items to their owners.
- Celebrate a successful project.

The project manager should ensure that someone handles completion of all items and that he or she has the resources to accomplish the work.

You should next close the contracts. If your project included an agreement with users of the services, signatures on the user acceptance form demonstrate that the contract is complete. A formal approval document officially validates that deliverables met acceptance criteria. Acceptance criteria should be reviewed and mapped back to the requirements and scope document. Formal acceptance is the legal acknowledgment that the deliverables have been supplied as intended. It is used to certify that the project has been completed, and to release the organization from any future obligations if the results transfer to another organization. Acceptance may come in an informal way, such as when the project is paid for and users experience the results of the project over time.

Depending on the terms of the contract, you may have other tasks to perform, such as to support the project's deliverables or to perform a follow-up in a few months. If you set up contracts with vendors, confirm that the other parties did what they were supposed to do. Then perform the steps to close those contracts as well.

The financial aspects of a project need attention in the closing stages. The project manager usually has responsibility for the budget and needs to ensure that costs are accounted for in the final statement. Sometimes organizations are unprepared for the extent to which small expenses become surprising amounts. If invoices are paid later than the contract requires, your project may incur unnecessary additional charges. Some of these charges can be high enough to send your project over budget at the last minute. This is one of the few costs project managers can avoid. Records of purchases shown on orders, delivery notes, and payments made against invoices are required. Discrepancies should be explained, and evidence provided when possible. A financial audit and arrangements for unpaid invoices and remaining assets or materials may be necessary.

For most projects, you will keep the financial books open for a short time, usually a few months after the project is complete. It is easy to process follow-up expenses, such as support. One way to prevent erroneous charges is to close all the accounting codes except those related to follow-up activities.

As the team prepares to work on other activities, the project manager should notify the organization's human resources office to ensure that the necessary forms are filed and the requirements for termination are prepared. Make your visibility greater in this period than at any time since the beginning of the project, as your team may begin to disintegrate when the project nears completion. Maintain a high profile and assume a position of strong leadership during the closing phase of the project.

After the project is finished, it must be converted to its useful state and turned over to the people who handle its maintenance. There must be a defined date for the deliverables to be transferred to whomever is now responsible for them.

Duncan and Gerrard (2011) provide an example of how transference occurs and how an end date for a project is required. The University of Saskatchewan in Saskatoon, Saskatchewan, Canada, created a virtual reference service project. The project lasted three years but was still considered a pilot after that period. A lack of an end date caused problems for the project, as the authors explain:

> The temporary status proved challenging for planning, marketing, funding, and staffing the service. Although the administrators were aware that marketing the service would likely increase its use, they were reluctant to do so, in case user expectations were created for a service that might cease to exist by the next academic year (p. 282).

After project sponsorship from a new dean, a push for library-wide integrated programs, and the creation of a taskforce to address the latter objective, the virtual service was assimilated into the reference duties. In other words, the project was formally completed and transitioned into ongoing operations of the academic library.

Closedown should be the final phase of every project. It requires careful planning. At this point the team delivers its results to the sponsor and stakeholders and then examines its performance. It is a shame if a successful project is left in a disordered condition when the team members transition to other areas of work. Once the purpose of the project has been achieved, closure tasks seem tedious, but they are necessary. Senior executives are inclined to gloss over this phase since they are unaccustomed to closing activities. Being action-oriented people, they are eager to move on without looking back once a job is finished. But reflection is indispensable to the ability to improve projects in the future.

Obtain stakeholder acceptance and verify satisfaction in a formalized way. Just as a formal kick-off meeting communicates project initiation, a ceremonial session where you secure satisfaction and acceptance signals project completion in a positive way.

7.4 PRODUCING FINAL REPORTS

The type and structure of the reports used to keep everyone informed depend on the project and the stakeholders. Externally funded projects have strict reporting rules. Grant-giving organizations will specify their reporting processes with forms and templates. For national and international projects, funders often expect you to disseminate information about the project. These stipulations ensure that results are shared, and demonstrate to your funders how you are spending their money.

It is worthwhile taking some time at the start of the project to identify the reporting requirements so you can set up systems to provide the necessary information for the reports. It will reduce last-minute panic as the project manager and team discover they have forgotten to collect the correct information.

Taking good notes for the duration of the project can benefit future projects and assist in the easier production of documentation. Records of research and initial planning are necessary, but make sure to note issues during the implementation phase of the project. Information on what went wrong and your solutions is critical in helping the next team create a better plan from the outset.

Other reasons for information dissemination include sharing good practices among the profession, publicizing your services, personal satisfaction, and career progression. One of the benefits of being a project manager is that you can take credit for successful projects and use them in your professional portfolio to help your career.

When drafting the final report, the tendency is to highlight good areas of the project and downplay the aspects that did not go as well as they should have. If the project was a great success, some measure of self-congratulations on the part of the project team is well earned. However, remember that someday you or others in your organization may perform a similar type of project, and an honest, factual final report may keep you from repeating a costly error.

Begin your closure report with an executive summary, including the most significant results. It should be a one- to two-page document summarizing the content for stakeholders who lack the time to read the entire report. This section covers the project overview and analysis at a high level. It presents the project concisely, which will be useful to you in refreshing your memory of the project in the future.

There are several other final project report elements to include as well (Table 7.2). In the remainder of the report, stress the accomplishments of the project team and recognize significant contributions individuals

Table 7.2 Final Project Report Elements

Element	Description
Executive summary	A summation of the longer report written so readers can become acquainted with the report without having to read it all
Project background	An outline of the project's history so that anomalies are understood
Major project activities	A description of the chief efforts of the project
Project results	A review of planned versus actual measurements to determine whether the variance would prevent a decision to close the project
Key project changes	An examination of scope changes with justifications for each change
Project challenges	A description of the most difficult parts of the project
Transition to operations	An analysis of how the project will shift into the operational sector of the organization
Matters outstanding	Any issues that remain unsettled

made to the project. Techniques used to get results are something you should highlight as well. Include retrospective project metrics and other performance information. A template for the final project report can be found in Appendix E.

You should also update documents related to your project to reflect the reality that exists in the project. The existence of accurate historical data can be of great value to project teams in the future. Update the project files to reflect final costs, schedules, functionality, and quality.

7.5 RECOGNIZING LESSONS LEARNED

When the project finishes, several outcomes for the project exist (Table 7.3). Hopefully, your project will be fully satisfactory or better. No matter what the project result, though, schedule a postevaluation to debrief and document the process so that the benefits of lessons learned can be shared. Ask yourself several questions as you reflect on the project (Table 7.4), and fill out a lessons-learned form to document your conclusions. A template can be found in Appendix E. Writing in the *Harvard Business Review*, Gulliver (1987) identified learning as an essential but overlooked benefit of project work: "If your company is like most, you spend thousands of hours planning an investment, millions of dollars implementing it—and nothing evaluating and learning from it" (p. 128).

Table 7.3 Project Outcomes

Outcome	Definition
Perfect	Exists only in theory. It involves no compromises and fulfills all expectations.
Outstanding	Is as close to perfect as can be expected in the real world. Deliverables exceed expectations.
Exceeds expectations	Delivers more than satisfactory results and is often either faster or cheaper than expected.
Fully satisfactory	Meets the expectations of on time, on budget, and in scope.
Barely adequate	Delivers the lowest level of expectations without being a failure.
Failure	Does not achieve the minimum acceptable outcome in one or more elements.
Catastrophe	Creates collateral damage.

Table 7.4 Lessons Learned Questions

- Did the project fulfill its vision?
- How good was the original scope?
- How well were the stakeholders satisfied with the project?
- Were all requirements met? If not, why not?
- How well were project objectives satisfied?
- How well did this project stay on schedule?
- Were any deliverables early or late? If so, why?
- How well did the team adjust to changes in the schedule?
- How well were resources estimated?
- How did the actual use of resources compare to the plan?
- How sound were our assumptions?
- How did changes in team member availability affect the project?
- How accurate were the time and cost estimates?
- How well did the team work together?
- How effectively did the stakeholders work together?
- What was the most frustrating part of the project?
- How could we do things differently next time to avoid this frustration?
- Were our meetings productive?
- What was the most satisfying part of the project?
- How were performance expectations set?
- How well were performance expectations satisfied?
- Where might have risk been anticipated better?
- What changes were made to the plan after implementation? Why?
- How well did our project methodology work?
- What project documents were most useful? Which, if any, were missing?
- How will the next project be improved?

Few organizations conduct reviews of their projects because of a reluctance to cause trouble and a desire to start the next project. If a review is skipped, however, mistakes will be repeated. The lessons-learned report identifies improvements that should be accommodated within a systemized approach. An organization can benefit from determining how future projects can be more efficient and effective. Team members can share what is learned more widely so that good practices can be adopted in other areas of work.

The postevaluation is an opportunity for discovery, not for criticism. Team members who fear they will be punished for past problems may try to hide them rather than help find better ways of handling them in the future. Avoid asking what went wrong, because it makes people defensive. A lessons-learned review should never be conducted from a punishment perspective.

Some project teams disband immediately, so the only chance to meet and reflect on the project as a whole will be at its completion. If that is your only chance to capture lessons learned, schedule time with your team that coincides with delivering your results. However, if you can wait a week or so after your project work concludes and schedule a separate activity for this purpose, you will get a more useful outcome. Waiting gives people a chance to reflect on the project as a whole rather than on the last part of the work, which tends to be stressful and affects how people feel about the project. Never delay more than two weeks, though, because you may have difficulty getting people to participate. Memories fade quickly.

A review of the internal functioning of the project will require examination of several areas. Was the project schedule on time? If delayed, how could this be improved in the future? How accurate were the resource estimates? What was the impact of resource availability on the project? How timely and precise was the reporting by the team? How would the team rate the individual performances of its members? What were the obstacles that impeded the work? How were conflicts resolved?

Documentation should include a description of achievements, activities, and challenges. An insightful description of the problems, issues, and concerns that the team encountered, with explanations of their resolutions, demonstrates effective project management.

In your evaluation, you will want to examine how tasks were accomplished and decide whether the best methods were used. If the practice was one that the team found useful, you need to review it so that it can be replicated in future projects. If an undertaking was achieved but the method could have been improved, you will want to list what aspects of the process should be analyzed and revamped for future projects. Determine why the revised method would be more effective and what the implications would be if you used it on the next project.

Team members should also contribute to lessons learned. Ask for direct feedback on particular aspects of the project. Does the team feel that the project met its intended goals? Discover whether team members agreed with how you approached issues that arose throughout the project. What would they have changed? Seek constructive criticism of the project and its management. Ask team members to point out what could have been done differently, then ask them for suggestions for alternative approaches.

Once the team identifies opportunities for improvement, communicate these to everyone who may gain from them. If the organization uses a methodology for project management, the project manager should include project successes and suggestions for methodology improvements in the final report.

The report is less valuable than the review itself. The first step of many projects should be to consider the lessons learned from the past, although this rarely happens. In most organizations, individual learning contributes to the improvement of organizational procedures more than the rectification of faults and anomalies when a project has been completed. However, the report may provide useful information to a new project's first risk identification meeting.

Even more helpful than the report is information dissemination. For large organizations, an intranet site may be an option to promote best practices gleaned from lessons learned. At a minimum, an email version of lessons learned sent to everyone on the project team, as well as to others involved in projects, is helpful. The project manager and key team members may also want to attend future project planning sessions to pass on lessons learned in person. This is especially useful when discussing risks, as the project manager may have input to situations similar to those that he or she encountered during the project.

For project managers, it is also helpful to perform a self-evaluation (Table 7.5). What lessons have you learned from managing the project? Did you improve your skills? How did you handle conflict in the project? Taking time for reflection gives an opportunity to improve your competence in the future.

Table 7.5 Project Management Skills Self-Evaluation

- How well did I deal with team members?
- How well did I communicate throughout the project?
- Did I keep stakeholders informed of the project's progress?
- Did I maintain the schedule?
- Was I flexible enough to alter the plans when needed?
- How well did I deal with conflict?
- Did I foresee risks? How well did I respond to them?
- How well did I monitor the project?
- Did I fulfill the objectives of the project?
- If not, could I have prevented project failure or was it out of my control?
- Did I have contingency plans?
- Did I make the right decision to utilize or not use contingency plans?
- What new project management skills did I learn?
- What would I change about this project? What would I keep the same?

Lessons learned give everyone a chance to reflect on what has been accomplished, what went right, what went wrong, and how the outcome might have been improved. Such reflections are the core of organizational learning that should be shared with other projects sponsored by the organization.

7.6 REWARDING THE TEAM

A successful project may conclude with satisfied users, pleased stakeholders, and a proud team. Since the team will disband once the project activities are complete, hold a party while it is still intact. A celebration of success demonstrates confidence in the project. A project's end provides an opportunity to thank people who have contributed to its success: both team members and many other individuals who supplied resources during the project's life cycle.

Celebratory events are motivating factors for the team, giving momentum in the later stages of a long project. Some teams celebrate each milestone review. Public announcements can also be effective. Parties and pronouncements are opportunities to acknowledge the efforts of the team and contribute to keeping morale high.

Acknowledging those who helped you achieve success is not only a nice thing to do. It is a strong building block for your future as well as the organization's. People who work hard and make significant contributes can become demotivated if their work is unrecognized. This damages the effectiveness of the organization. At a more personal level, if you gain a reputation as someone who appreciates a job well done, you are more likely to garner the people and resources you want for future projects.

Thank people face to face if possible. For remote team members, make a personal phone call, send a card, or write a thoughtful email. Find at least one asset in particular to comment on for each individual as a way to reinforce your appreciation. Chances are that you will work again with at least some of the people who were on your team, and how you exit this project will make a difference when you next meet.

The end of a project can be an emotional experience for team members. The schedule will indicate when they complete their tasks, and many move to other work before the project is completed. Team members will plan their futures concerning the anticipated completion of the project. For some there will be a sense of loss, but others may be excited by new prospects offered in their next assignment. In some cases opportunities may occur because of skills and experiences gained through working on the soon-to-end project.

One issue that surfaces near a project's end is that the project is absent from the daily working lives of team members. As a result, they may feel unhappy in their work; they may become unmotivated, lose interest in their jobs, and seek other roles. Sometimes the recognition that this transition is taking place can reassure team members so they can adapt. Project managers who are aware of this process ensure that team members experience a period where they reengage with their daily roles. In some instances team members realize that they enjoy projects, and become committed to developing their careers in project-based work.

Closure timing may be a delicate matter, as some staff members will leave before the project is finished and others may not have other jobs in place. The project is incomplete until closure has been completed, and it is helpful if the people managing final activities are untroubled about their futures. Planning in advance can reduce the stress of the last stages of the project.

7.7 HANDLING TRANSITION

A formal transition period helps people through the psychological issues that go hand in hand with work–life transitions, which is important when team members have devoted themselves to a project.

As a project nears completion, the team should transfer deliverables to their recipients. Deliverables are not always tangible products, and handover may require support or training. The outcomes and deliverables need to be either handed over or accounted for if anything is missing.

Arrangements should be made for any conditions that are necessary for the transfer of responsibility to be completed. Handover is usually a formal procedure where the person responsible for accepting the delivery examines everything and signs off that the project is complete. This process ensures unconditional agreement that the project outcomes have been achieved.

In some projects, handovers occur before the project's conclusion—often between different teams working on sequential tasks. A record should be made in case a dispute arises about where responsibly lies. Accommodating additional tasks in the late stages can be difficult, because staff allocated to the team will often have made arrangements to move to different work after the completion of the majority of their project work.

Organizations frequently commission projects with little consideration for the maintenance burden that will occur after a project is completed.

Most team members will not be involved after the final delivery of the project, and they may disinterested in the sustainability of the project. You must overcome this apathy and make sure that maintenance is planned so that the results of the project may be used for a substantial amount of time.

At the end of a project, training may be required. If training is necessary before users can benefit from the outcomes, this should have been anticipated and built into the project plans. The team should train the recipients of the project how to use and maintain deliverables, through manuals, workshops, hands-on exercises, or a combination of approaches. When new owners have accepted the work as part of their day-to-day operations, the project has turned over to its recipients.

Depending on the type of project and deliverables, the team may offer extended support. This usually requires the project and operational teams to work together as the new technology is implemented, so that the operational team can learn from the project team about the deliverables.

Get the necessary information from contracted or temporary team members, including their computer passwords and file locations. Make sure that all data for team members who were only hired for the project is accessible, including personal information needed for tax-related documents. If team members are leaving after the project ends, retrieve their badges, security cards, and office keys. If your organization lacks a formal exit interview process, arrange an informal meeting to give and receive feedback and collect the organizational property.

7.8 CREATING PROJECT ARCHIVES

Every project produces documents, such as meeting minutes, budget data, and performance evaluations. These materials should be collected and stored in both paper and electronic formats. These archives represent the project's official history. The project manager should ensure that project records are retrievable in the future. Documents confirming that contractual obligations were completed should be kept with the project plans, budgets, and relevant staff records. The minutes of major meetings are also retained so that agreements made can be reviewed. All versions of the plan with notes related to changes should be kept as well. Include the original and final schedules, original budget and final expenditures, all progress reports, and correspondence, along with other critical information that helps you recount the course of the project.

For paper storage, the location should be central to or near the project, in a reasonably accessible yet secure place. Copies of project documentation should be filed here, with the possible exception of technical manuals, which may have to be kept at the project work site. The organization's servers, intranet site, project database, or website can provide convenient access to all these documents electronically.

To review your records effectively, consolidate your materials. Highlight specific documents as you proceed through the project, noting when critical decisions were made and what processes were sanctioned.

Even though the project work is complete, there will most likely be further changes that warrant follow-up projects. By using the deliverables, you can identify improvement opportunities, features to be added, and functions to be modified. The project documentation is the foundation for the follow-up projects.

You will want to create an archives of the project because the types of projects you manage will be similar. Completed projects are a terrific source of information for future projects. However, this only works if the data and other documentation from them are archived so that they can be retrieved and used. You never know when you might have a situation in a future project that you know you have already solved in a previous one, but you may have forgotten how exactly. Referring to the archives can save you hours of work. Estimated and actual durations and costs for each activity on completed projects are particularly valuable for estimating these variables on future projects. The archives can also serve as a training resource for new project managers and the project team.

Additionally, you may create systems and procedures to streamline your work. Developing templates, forms, checklists, processes, and other tools to simplify repetitive tasks is a powerful benefit that the project management methodology can give you.

Creating project archives can also maintain knowledge within the organization. Knowledge transfer is an effective learning and development tool, but is often lost if organizations hire temporary workers or contractors for the project. The challenge is to identify all knowledge transfer practices that can impart insight from one project to another, regardless of where the practitioners reside.

When the project manager has submitted the final reports, archived the materials, and worked with the team and sponsors to make sure that everything has been completed, the project is officially concluded.

Conclusion

Some projects are ambitious in their social, economic, and political impacts. Others are less grand. Some require advances in systems, and others deploy proven technologies and best practices. Some projects are wild successes, while others fail.

Projects are the way in which human creativity is most effectively harnessed to achieve tangible, lasting results. Building a pyramid, painting a ceiling, or founding a nation requires vision, planning, and the coordinated effort of a team—the fundamental features of projects.

Project management is one of the most difficult jobs to perform. Positive performance is the only way to maintain your position as a project manager. Project management is a multifarious process that begins with knowledge and compounds with experience.

Project management is iterative. With practice, you improve your proficiency, but you never master the process. Stakeholders cause problems, scopes creep, and resources may be unavailable when you need them the most. Project management allows the project to be balanced at all times. Project managers assess the situation and gain control of projects before they become uncontrollable.

Adhering to proven project management practices reduces risk, cuts costs, and improves the success rates of projects. Organizations are likely to nurture a project management culture when they understand the value it brings and how projects drive change. Organizations also recognize that when projects fail, they are less likely to achieve strategic goals. Archives, libraries, and museums should acknowledge the value of people who are resourceful, have strategic insight, and champion knowledge development and transfer as essential to performance improvement. Utilizing project management makes success possible.

Project management is closely tied to change management because projects, by their very nature, cause change. Change management is the implementation of planned alterations to established missions, objectives, or procedures within an organization. It typically refers to the intentional processes undertaken by organizations in response to internal needs, but it may also include strategies for reacting to external events. Lasting change incorporates the mission, goals, and objectives of the institution. Simultaneous changes in structures, systems, and people leads to changes in the culture of the organization. As with project management, change management requires that stakeholders understand the rationale for change and that they are engaged and supportive of new solutions.

Information professionals need to be capable of managing and participating in projects and should be able to anticipate and support the resulting organizational change. Indeed, change management is crucial to the success of projects involving the integration of new information technologies. For example, it is not enough to implement a new content management system and incorporate it into organizational functions. It must also be accepted and applied by the creators and users of documents, which involves the application of change management skills.

Weingand (1997) writes:

> Too often, organizational culture is rooted in tradition and habit, and change is often an unwelcome visitor. Yet, change is today's one constant, and no organization can escape its presence and effects. Whether regarded as an opportunity or as a threat, the specter of change sits on every organization's board of directors; the library is no exception (p. 7).

In the world in which most information professionals work, innovation and the change that comes as a result have not always been welcomed in organizations focused on maintaining the status quo of previous generations. Memory institutions like libraries, archives, and museums adhere to traditions, which can sometimes make change difficult. Schreiber and Shannon (2001) write:

> The hyper speed of change in information services now demands libraries that are lean, mobile and strategic. They must be lean to meet expanding customer expectations within the confines of limited budgets; mobile to move quickly and easily with technological and other innovations; and strategic to anticipate and plan for market changes (p. 36).

Additionally, information professionals work in environments that include complex classification systems, technical infrastructures, and organizational configurations. It is tempting to view these conditions as constraining. However, thinking about organizations structurally overlooks the challenge that is central to the information profession: deploying information services in ways that change the communities libraries, archives, and museums serve. Information professionals are increasingly called upon to facilitate the reconceptualization and redesign of services. As project managers, team members, or stakeholders, information professionals are involved in projects that change organizations.

As a result, Doan and Kennedy (2009) note that information professionals have: come to view change as the means of accomplishing significant goals, recognizing that our organizations must keep pace with user needs, acknowledging that we do indeed have information competitors and that we are part of organizations and therefore must align with larger objectives than our own. It is essential to innovate to continue to be meaningful (p. 349).

Munduate and Media (2009) state similarly, "Organizations will only survive if they have the flexibility to react to the constantly changing demands and if they are adept enough at redirecting, orientating, and exploiting their resources efficiently" (p. 299). Successful projects are one way to create an environment that embraces change as an opportunity, not as a threat.

Present situations in organizations are largely the result of decisions made in the past. Information professionals should not allow themselves to become captives to previous decisions. They must question decisions made in the past and effect changes that would position the organization well in the future. Innovation and the systematic abandonment of obsolete practices is a critical factor in the renewal and growth of memory institutions.

Archives, libraries, and museums require the services of a cross-trained, highly integrated staff of information professionals with project management knowledge. They act as facilitators, catalysts for change, and managers for complex information systems. Project managers bring chaos to order and blurred vision to clear reality. As with most projects, you and your team have learned many new tactics that you will be able to use in future project assignments. As you have discovered throughout the volume, project management is never dull. Hopefully, with the knowledge you have gained from reading this book, you will eagerly continue your project management journey.

Project Management Considerations

INITIATION

- What is the purpose of the project?
- Who is the sponsor of this project?
- Who are the stakeholders? Why are they interested in the project?
- How will the project charter be developed?
- Who will approve the project charter?
- How will the project scope be defined? Who will validate it?
- What departments and external organizations will be involved?
- How will the project be staffed?
- If hiring is required, how will it be done? Who is responsible?
- For team members who report to other managers, how will commitments be documented?
- What are the responsibilities of the team members?
- Who will manage training for team members?

PLANNING AND SCHEDULING

- Will a project methodology be used?
- What level of planning detail is appropriate for this project?
- What is the agenda for the kick-off meeting? Where and when will it be held?
- How will you plan for risk?
- What planning meetings will you hold? When and how will you conduct them?
- What process will you use to make changes to the plan?
- Who approves the plan?
- At what level of detail will you document your work breakdown structure?
- What information will you define for each activity?
- Will you conduct periodic plan reviews? How frequently?

- In addition to the project manager, who will plan the project?
- What are the roles and responsibilities of the planning participants?
- Who will review the overall plan?
- What techniques will you use for planning and scheduling?
- Will you use a software application for scheduling and tracking?

VENDORS

- How will you determine if you will need to use vendors? Who should be involved in the process?
- What approvals will you require? What support will you need, and who will provide it?
- Who will create the request for proposals?
- Who will manage communications with potential vendors?
- Who will evaluate the proposals?
- Who will select vendors and negotiate the contracts?
- Who will handle managing relationships with vendors?

STATUS UPDATES

- What status information will you collect for the project?
- How frequently will you gauge project conditions?
- What method will you use to get statuses from team members?
- How will you validate data?
- Who will compare the status with the project baseline and assess project progress?

METRICS

- What status-based measures will you use for this project?
- How will metrics be defined and documented?
- Do the measures have validated baselines or other limits?
- What process will you use to evaluate the measures?
- What post-project measures will you collect?
- How will you use retrospective measures to improve your next project?

INFORMATION SYSTEMS

- Where will status data and other metrics data be stored?
- Who will supervise establishing the information system? How will information be organized?

- Who will maintain and have change access to the system?
- What specific documents and other information will be in the system?
- How long will data in the system be archived following the project?

MEETINGS

- What meetings will be held for this project? What are their objectives?
- Who will determine the meetings' agendas?
- Is the length of the sessions as short as practical considering the schedule?
- Who will lead the meetings? Who will facilitate them?
- Who will document the meetings and distribute minutes?
- What ground rules will you use for meetings?
- What other meetings, if any, will be required for this project?

TEAMWORK

- How will your team make decisions?
- What process will you use to track issues and problems?
- Where will issues and action items be managed?
- How will you manage conflicts between team members?
- What activities will you do to enhance teambuilding?
- What training and development for team members are necessary for this project?
- How frequently will you meet one-on-one with each team member?
- How will you resolve performance problems with team members?

COMMUNICATION

- What will be in your communications plan?
- What communication methods will you use for the project?
- How will you encourage frequent interactions and informal conversations among team members?

QUALITY ASSURANCE

- Are procedures relating to ensuring the quality of your deliverables well documented and used?
- How frequently do you conduct reviews to ensure that the processes continue to serve their need?
- What is your procedure for evaluating a process and proposing process improvements?

REPORTING

- What reporting will be required?
- Who will create reports? How often?
- Who will distribute the reports? Who will receive the reports?
- Will specialized reporting be needed for the sponsor or stakeholders?
- Will reports for issue tracking, scope changes, risk management, or other aspects be required for this project?
- What criteria will be used to determine if problem reports need to be generated?

SCOPE CONTROL

- What scope change management process will you use?
- How will you document proposed changes?
- What process will you use to analyze submitted changes?
- Who will be involved in making decisions to accept or reject changes for your project?
- How will you communicate change decisions?
- For accepted changes, who will update the documents?

CONTROL

- Who will be involved in assessing progress?
- How will you evaluate schedule progress?
- How much cost or resource overrun can you tolerate before changing the project?
- What metrics related to quality are relevant for this project?
- How will you determine progress for outsourced work?
- How frequently will you reassess risks? How will you document potential problems?

PROJECT REPORTING

- How often will this project require plan reports?
- Who will schedule and prepare the reports?
- Which team members need to participate in the reports?
- Will the sponsor or other stakeholders participate in the reports?
- How will the results be documented? Who will receive the results?

CANCELLATION

- What criteria will be used to determine whether to stop this project?
- Who decides whether to change or cancel the project?
- What process will you use to close a canceled project? What activities and deliverables are required?

CLOSURE

- What process will you use for testing and scope verification?
- What sign-offs are required? Who must validate successful completion?
- When will you determine the lessons learned? Who will participate?
- What final reports are required?
- What process will you use to close out the vendors' contracts?
- How will you commemorate the conclusion of the project with your team?
- What rewards are possible for those who contributed to the project?

APPENDIX B

Further Reading

This section offers books and websites you can access for more information on various project management topics. The resources range from refresher material, which is useful to consider when you are starting a new project, to pointers toward more advanced information. In complex projects, you may find that you want some more rigorous tools at your disposal.

Also included are resources relating to personal productivity and people management. One feature that is familiar to project managers is organization. Being able to keep on top of details is a useful skill to develop, and the resources here will point you in the right direction. Although people management is often not a direct responsibility of the project manager, many of these tools will be useful if you are managing the human component of your projects as well as the technical or work components. Developing these kinds of soft skills can equip you with a better range of techniques for dealing with your sponsor, stakeholders, and project team.

BOOKS

Allan, B., 2004. *Project Management: Tools and Techniques for Today's ILS Professional*. Facet, London.

Allen provides a practical approach to project management as part of change management. The book offers case studies from the library and archives sector, and provides tested methods for managing projects.

Allen, D., 2014. *Getting Things Done: The Art of Stress-Free Productivity*. Penguin Books, New York.

Getting Things Done is a comprehensive system for personal productivity. Allen promotes ways to capture to-do lists methodically to become better organized and less stressed.

Anderson, D.J., 2010. *Kanban: Successful Evolutionary Change for Your Technology Business*. Blue Hole Press, Sequim, WA.

This book is a guide to starting Kanban, a practical approach to implementing lean software development.

Berkun, S., 2005. *The Art of Project Management.* O'Reilly, Sebastopol, CA.

Focusing on the soft skills needed for project management work, Berkun offers a personal account of the lessons he has learned as an experienced manager of software and web development.

Cagle, R., 2005. *Your Successful Project Management Career.* AMACOM, New York.

This book offers a structured view of project management that is useful for novice project managers. While it is not formulated to any particular industry, it provides some differences between small, medium, large, and program-sized projects.

Carpenter, J., 2010. *Project Management in Libraries, Archives and Museums: Working with Government and Other External Partners.* Chandos, Oxford.

This practical handbook guides users on project management techniques for academic and cultural heritage institutions. The focus is on managing projects involving public sector and external partners. It covers diverse project management issues, including choosing the most appropriate method for the institution or project, using management applications in project development and implementation, providing project sustainability, assessing risk management, and evaluating outcomes.

Cohen, A.R., Bradford, D.L., 2005. *Influence Without Authority*, second ed. John Wiley & Sons, New York.

The book's message is that to succeed, you must learn to influence others. Although you may not have authority as a project manager, you can have enough power to make things happen using techniques outlined in this book.

DeMarco, T., Lister, T., 2014. *Peopleware: Productive Projects and Teams*, third ed. Addison-Wesley, Upper Saddle River, NJ.

Peopleware was one of the first books aimed at technical workers transitioning to managers, and it offers advice for managing teams with relevant, real-world examples. It includes insightful essays on the human side of project management.

DeMarco, T., Lister, T., 2003. *Waltzing with Bears: Managing Risk on Software Projects.* Dorset House Publishing, New York, NY.

The book challenges readers to examine their organizations to determine the current level of risk management, how to improve it, and how to build accountability from stakeholders involved in projects. It has useful risk management techniques that are applicable beyond software projects.

Dresang, E.T., Gross, M., Holt, L.E., 2006. *Dynamic Youth Services through Outcome-Based Planning and Evaluation.* American Library Association, Chicago.

The authors developed an assessment strategy for youth services at the St. Louis Public Library that makes sense to practitioners. The method lends itself particularly well to the evaluations required for grant-funded projects.

Fagan, J.C., Keach, J.A., 2009. *Web Project Management for Academic Libraries.* Chandos, Oxford.

This collection of practical solutions outlines best practices for managing successful projects related to an academic library website. It will help web project managers plan, engage stakeholders, and lead organizations through change. Although the subject's scope is narrow, many of the techniques in the book can be applied to similar projects encountered by information professionals.

Fisher, R., Sharp, A., 1998. *Getting It Done: How to Lead When You're Not in Charge.* HarperBusiness, New York.

This book focuses on principled negotiation and influencing others in the workplace.

Fisher, R., Ury, W.L., 2012. *Getting to Yes: Negotiating Agreement Without Giving In,* third ed. Random House, London.

Since its original publication nearly 30 years ago, this book has helped millions to negotiate effectively. It offers strategies for coming to mutually acceptable agreements in every type of conflict, especially project management.

Garrett, D., Bradbary, D., 2005. *Herding Chickens: Innovative Techniques for Project Management.* Harbor Light Press, San Francisco.

The book contains unconventional techniques for successful project management from a seasoned professional.

Harvard Business Review Press, 2014. *Managing Projects.* Harvard Business Review Press, Boston, MA.

As part of the 20-Minute Manager series, this book offers a concise, easy-to-follow overview of project management. Concepts include discovering what stakeholders expect from a project, how to schedule realistically, how to form the right team, and how to assess the project. Although it is a short book, it provides enough information to start a project successfully.

Heerkens, G., 2007. *Project Management: 24 Steps to Help You Master Any Project*. McGraw-Hill, New York.

This useful guide offers an introduction to new project managers and a refresher for experienced leaders. Heerkens's real-life experience provides a practical approach to project management.

Kendrick, T., 2014. *The Project Management Tool Kit: 100 Tips and Techniques for Getting the Job Done Right*, third ed. AMACOM/American Management Association, New York.

This handy guide provides practical techniques for project management, including checklists, charts, and tools.

Lopp, M., 2013. *Managing Humans: Biting and Humorous Tales of a Software Engineering Manager*. Apress, Berkeley, CA.

This book, containing anecdotes from a software engineering manager, provides approaches for dealing with managing people in different project scenarios.

O'Connell, F., 2011. *What You Need to Know about Project Management*. Capstone Publishing, West Sussex, UK.

This short, engaging book offers a practical approach to project management. It covers the basics of project management while providing tips for handling project management challenges.

Project Management Institute, 2013. *A Guide to the Project Management Book of Knowledge (PMBOK Guide)*, fifth ed. Project Management Institute, Newton Square, PA.

Comprehensive and detailed, this book is best used as a reference and an aid to passing your project management professional exams.

Schmaltz, D.A., 2003. *The Blind Men and the Elephant: Mastering Project Work*. Berrett-Koehler Publishers, San Francisco.

Using the familiar metaphor of six blind men who fail to describe an elephant to each other, the book seeks out the cause of difficulties in project work and how colleagues can create meaning from their experiences.

Schwaber, K., 2009. *Agile Project Management with SCRUM*. O'Reilly Media, New York.

SCRUM, an agile software development method, is critical for technical work and can be applied to nontechnical projects with good results. This book introduces SCRUM to the uninitiated, and teaches readers to manage projects with agility.

BLOGS AND WEBSITES

43Folders: 43folders.com

43Folders, run by Merlin Mann, is dedicated to the Getting Things Done approach. The site provides an in-depth understanding of the tools of GTD.

LibraryProject.Info: www.libraryproject.info

Michael Perry, the collection services project manager at Northwestern University Library, writes a concise blog on the usage of project management in library settings.

Lifehacker: www.lifehacker.com

The site offers updates every day with tips, tricks, and techniques for hacking your life and making you more productive.

Rands in Repose: randsinrepose.com

Rands is the *alter ego* of Michael Lopp, who wrote *Managing Humans*, listed above. This site is worth reading for its helpful advice, as well as for the enduring sense that everything can be fixed.

UCLA Library Special Collections Digital Project Toolkit: http://library.ucla.edu/special-collections/programs-projects/digital-projects-special-collections

The Digital Project Toolkit was developed throughout the course of several digital projects that occurred at UCLA's Center for Primary Research and Training from 2013 to 2015. It is designed to support digital projects in archives and libraries. Focused on collaborative digital humanities, digitization, and digital platform development projects, the toolkit serves as a reference for institutions planning and implementing digital projects by providing project management templates, guidelines, and examples.

VIDEOS

Lynda.com

Lynda.com offers video courses on software, creative, and business skills taught by industry experts. A suite of 40 project management courses offered by the Project Management Institute can be chosen to keep your Project Management Practitioner certification current. The tutorials also allow those who are new to project management to learn the fundamentals of the craft.

Calculating Earned Value with Aileen Ellis

This Lynda.com video explains the calculations behind earned-value management, one of the most critical project metrics. Using two examples (a construction project and a system upgrade), Ellis shows how earned-value metrics can help you calculate current performance, interpret the results, and forecast future performance.

APPENDIX C

Software Programs

Many software programs can manage projects effectively. Scheduling tools and project management software range from the simple to the complex. The level of sophistication and the types of project management techniques that you use will determine which software product you should choose. Often the best tool is dictated by the software that team members are comfortable using. When you are choosing project management tools, make sure you are selecting something that is both functional and will be adopted wholeheartedly by the people involved in the project. Below is a list of some of the programs yon can find online.

Artemis: http://www.aisc.com/
Basecamp: https://basecamp.com/
Central Desktop: https://www.centraldesktop.com/
Clarizen: http://www.clarizen.com/
Computer Associates: http://www.ca.com/
Copper Project: http://copperproject.com/
dotProject: http://dotproject.net/
FastTrack Schedule: http://www.aecsoftware.com/project-management-software/fasttrack-schedule-win/
GanttProject: http://www.ganttproject.biz/
Gathersplace: http://www.gatherspace.com/
Genius Project: http://www.geniusproject.com/
InLoox: http://www.inloox.com/
LiquidPlanner: http://www.liquidplanner.com/
Microsoft Project: https://products.office.com/en-us/Project
Microsoft SharePoint: https://products.office.com/en-us/SharePoint
MinuteMan: http://www.minuteman-systems.com/index.htm
OmniPlan: https://www.omnigroup.com/applications/omniplan
OpenAir: http://www.openair.com/
Planisware: https://www.planisware.com/
Planview Enterprise: http://www.planview.com/
Primavera: http://www.primavera.com/
Project Insight: http://www.projectinsight.net/
Project Kickstart: http://www.projectkickstart.com/
Project.net: http://www.project.net/

ProjectPartner: http://www.projectpartner.com/
ProjectPier: http://www.andrexa.com/
Projectplace: https://www.projectplace.com/
ProWorkFlow: https://www.proworkflow.com/
RationalPlan: http://www.rationalplan.com/
RiskyProject: http://www.intaver.com/
SmartDraw: http://www.smartdraw.com/
TaskJuggler: http://www.taskjuggler.org/
Trac: http://trac.edgewall.org/
Track+: http://www.trackplus.com/en/
Tracker: http://www.acentre.com/
Twproject: https://www.twproject.com/
Viewpath: http://www.viewpath.com/
VPMi: http://www.vcsonline.com/
Wrike: http://www.wrike.com/
Zoho Projects: http://www.zoho.com/projects/

APPENDIX D

Glossary

8/80 Rule A project management rule stating that tasks should take no more than 80 hours and no fewer than 8 hours of labor to create. It prevents work packages from being too large or too small to manage.

Action meeting A meeting designed for getting something done or making decisions, followed by action items or minutes.

Activity The work performed to achieve a result.

Activity description A statement that specifies what should be done to achieve a result.

Activity-on-arrow A network diagram showing a sequence of activities; an arrow represents each activity with a circle representing an event at each end.

Activity-on-node A network diagram showing the sequence of activities, with each activity represented by a box or circle (a node) interconnected with arrows to indicate the precedence of work.

Actual cost The cost that a project has incurred, including labor, equipment, material, and indirect costs.

Actual duration The length of time between when a task started and the status date if the task is not yet complete.

Actual to date (ATD) The amount of time or budget that has been spent to date.

Adjourning In Bruce Tuckman's model of team development, adjourning is the first phase of development, marked by completing the task and breaking up the team.

Agile A methodology that uses quick execution, daily meetings, and adaptability to changes. The model uses small increments of planning and implementation of the requirements.

Allocation The percentage of a person's time that is assigned to a task.

Analogous estimating technique A means to approximate the time and cost needed to complete a deliverable by comparing it to a deliverable with similar characteristics.

Area of responsibility The person or department responsible for the execution of a task as part of the project.

As late as possible (ALAP) A dependency relationship where the finish of the predecessor task will be scheduled as late in the schedule as possible.

As soon as possible (ASAP) A dependency relationship where the start of the successor task will be scheduled as close to the finish of the predecessor task as possible.

Assumption An underlying belief supporting a budget, schedule, or another effort that involves calculating future requirements.

Audit A detailed review of the project by people outside the team or outside the organization.

Authority The power given to people to use resources to reach objectives.

Backward pass calculation A method of working backward through a network from the latest event to the beginning event to calculate event late times.

Baseline The original and stakeholder-approved plan for the schedule and cost for a project, including any approved changes.

Baseline cost The project costs in the baseline plan used to calculate earned-value measures and project cost performance.

Benefit An improvement to an organization, such as increased revenues, reduced costs, or enhanced employee morale.

Body language Nonverbal communication such as hand gestures and eye movements.

Bottleneck Any task on the critical path that causes the work after it to amass.

Bottom-up estimating A method used to evaluate the time and cost needed to complete activities at a low level of detail.

Brainstorming A technique used to gather ideas for a solution to a problem, without any immediate evaluation of these ideas.

Budget An estimate of a project's costs and expenses; the means of financial monitoring based on planned and actual costs and expenses.

Budget at completion (BAC) The estimated cost of the project at completion, including actual costs to date and estimated costs from today until the finish date.

Budget estimate A value based on the details of the project scope. It ranges from −10% to +25% on average.

Budget variance The result of when actual expenses are higher or lower than budgeted amounts.

Business analyst An individual who identifies the business needs of the organization, helps determine solutions to problems, completes requirements development, and performs requirements management. The business analyst also facilitates communication between end users, stakeholders, and the project team.

Business case A proposal for organizational improvement. It contains the goals of the project and how those goals support the goals of the organization, as well as a fiscal analysis and estimate.

Business continuity plan A plan designed to get an organization through a disaster. Its goal is to help restore the organization to normal as soon as possible.

Business impact analysis The process of analyzing the impact on an organization of several kinds of disasters.

Business process management A process used to describe how work flows through an organization; the basis for preparation of a flowchart and assigning tasks to the project team.

Business requirements The requirements that refer to business functions of the project, such as project, financial, or change management, and how the project will satisfy the business needs of the users.

Buy-in A way of securing personal or organizational agreement with project goals or management methods.

Calendar The arrangement of working days, together with holidays, vacations, and overtime periods, used to determine dates on which work will be completed.

Cash hole The most money that will be invested in the project at any point. Also known as the maximum exposure.

Change control A process for managing the consequences of variations in a project.

Change control board A group of stakeholders who approve or reject requested changes to project baselines.

Change management The process of managing organizational change in a way that disrupts business as little as possible.

Change management plan A document that describes the change management process for a project.

Change order A document that sanctions a change in the project.

Change request The description of a change in project requirements, which, if approved, usually affects the scope or quality and may affect the cost and time dimensions of a project.

Closing The project phase in which the final activities are performed and the project is signed off.

Closing process The process of accepting the project as complete, documenting the performance, and releasing resources.

Co-location The practice of placing all the key team members near one another.

Collaboration The practice of working with others to achieve goals.

Communication plan A plan that describes how project communication will take place, listing the relevant meetings, emails, and updates.

Constraint A limitation related to time, scope, or cost that affects the project in some way.

Contingency An amount of money, time, or both that is set aside for situations that cannot be completely defined in advance, such as using more time than originally planned to correct defects.

Contingency planning The act of planning for project risks and disruptions.

Control The procedures for monitoring progress against a plan so that corrections are taken when a deviation occurs.

Controlling process The process of comparing actual progress to the plan, analyzing the differences, evaluating alternatives, and taking corrective steps if necessary.

Core process The project management process that must be performed in approximately the same order in all projects.

Corrective action The steps taken to bring future project performance in line with planned project performance.

Cost The expenditures for people, equipment, and materials.

Cost baseline The agreed-upon costs associated with the project that form the expected total cost of the project.

Cost-benefit analysis A form of comparison between the costs and benefits, planned or actual, to determine a project's financial viability.

Cost control The procedures involved in controlling fiscal changes related to a project.

Cost estimating The development of a cost approximation of resources needed to complete the project activities.

Cost management The process of monitoring project cost data to determine performance and variance from the planned cost targets.

Cost management plan A plan that describes how cost variances will be managed.

Cost of quality The expenditures incurred to ensure quality, including quality planning, control, assurance, and rework.

Cost performance index (CPI) The ratio of budgeted costs to actual costs.

Cost resource A resource type for expenses, such as travel, training, and rentals, that are not related to hours worked or quantities consumed.

Cost-to-complete The amount that a project component will cost until the project is finished.

Cost-to-date The amount that a project component has cost to date.

Cost variation The difference between the budgeted and actual costs of work performed. If the cost variance is positive, the project is under budget.

Crashing An attempt to reduce activity or total project duration, usually by adding resources.

Crisis management The way that an organization responds to disaster to lessen or avoid adverse effects.

Critical path The sequential path of activities essential for completion of a project.

Critical path method A network diagramming method that shows the longest series of activities in a project, thereby determining the earliest completion time for the project.

Critical path schedule The longest chain of deliverables in a project.

Current state The present condition of a project, as opposed to its future state.

Customer relationship management The software and systems that let users interact with clients.

Decision loop A process in which a decision may result in the process continuing or being sent back to be fixed.

Decision tree A tool used to analyze outcomes of a proposed course of action.

Decomposition The process of breaking down a work packet into smaller tasks to be used when developing the work breakdown structure.

Deliverable An end product that composes the project.

Delphi estimating technique A method used for developing a consensus about an estimate through surveys and meetings.

Dependency A relationship in which work on one task cannot be started or completed before another task has been finalized.

Dependent task A task that cannot start until other tasks are completed.

Deviation Any variation from planned performance, such as schedule, cost, quality, or scope of work.

Disaster recovery The plans made so that an organization continues to work after a disaster or a disruption to service.

Discovery The process of finding potential projects to undertake.

Dummy activity A zero-duration element in a network showing a logical linkage.

Duration The time it takes to complete an activity.

Earliest finish The earliest time that an action can be completed.

Earliest start The earliest time that an activity can be started.

Earned value A cost and schedule analysis tool designed to help you evaluate whether or not your project is on schedule and within budget.

Earned-value analysis A method of measuring performance by comparing baseline costs to how much has been spent and how much should have been spent for the completed work.

Effort The number of units of work to complete a task.

Effort-driven task A task whose total work does not vary as resources are added or removed.

End user The recipient of a project's deliverables.

Estimate An approximate calculation of the time or budget needed to achieve a particular task.

Estimate at completion (EAC) The forecast total cost at completion for a task or project.

Estimate to complete (ETC) The effort or cost left remaining on a task.

Event A point in time. An event is either achieved or not, whereas an activity can be partially complete.

Executing The project phase in which the plans are carried out and the majority of the actual work of the project is completed.

Executing process The process in which a project is launched and the plan is implemented.

Facilitator A person, usually a consultant or human resource trainer, who helps team members to work together effectively.

Fast-tracking The process of shortening the duration of a project by overlapping tasks that would normally be run sequentially, such as design and construction.

Favorable variance A condition when actual expenses are lower than budgeted for a period or activity.

Feasibility study Research conducted to determine each solution's likelihood of meshing with the business architecture and the organizational mission, and reaching financial, operational, and technical achievability.

Feedback The information derived from observation of activities that is used to analyze the status of the job and take corrective action if needed.

Finish date A date that a task is scheduled to be completed, based on the task's start date, duration, work calendars, and constraints.

Finish-to-finish A task relationship in which one task must finish at the same time as another.

Finish-to-start A task relationship in which one task must finish before another can begin.

Fit for purpose A process to determine the suitability of a service or product to meet the needs of its users.

Fixed cost A cost for a task that does not depend on the task duration.

Float A calculation of how much an activity can be delayed before it affects the finish date.

Flowchart A visual representation of a schedule that identifies the process, areas of responsibility, time requirements, and weak links.

Forecast An estimate of what is likely to happen in the future.

Forming In Bruce Tuckman's model of team development, forming is the first phase of development, marked by little agreement on team aims and a high level of dependence on the project manager.

Forward pass calculation An estimate determining the earliest start time for each activity in a network diagram.

Free float The amount of time that an activity can be delayed without an effect on other activities.

Free slack The amount of time a task can slip without delaying another task.

Functional manager A department manager responsible for the people who work in that department. The project manager works with functional managers to obtain resources for a project.

Future state The project's end point, when users assess work and disband.

Gantt chart A bar chart, developed by Henry L. Gantt, which indicates the time required to complete each activity in a project.

Gold plating A process of adding extra features that may drive up costs and alter schedules.

Handover The process by which a project is documented and responsibility is transferred to the ongoing operational or support team.

Human resource planning A process used to assign roles and responsibilities and generate a staffing management plan.

Hygiene agents From Herzberg's theory of motivation, these elements are the expectations all workers have: job security, a paycheck, safe working conditions, civil working relationships, and other basics associated with employment.

Implementation plan A plan that indicates what work will be done, when it will be performed, who will do the work, and how much it will cost.

Independent task This task is not reliant on other activities, and no other activities are reliant on this task being completed.

Inexcusable delay A postponement that is attributable to negligence on the part of a contractor and may incur penalty payments.

Information architect This role helps assess the data requirements of a project, identifies data assets, and helps the project team complete data modeling requirements.

Information distribution The process of making information available to stakeholders promptly.

Infrastructure analyst A position that designs the hardware, software, and technical infrastructure required for a project's application development, operation requirements, and ongoing solution.

Initiating The phase in which the project starts.

Initiating process The project management process in which the team commits to starting a project.

Intangible benefit A benefit that may not be easy to quantify, such as increased user satisfaction or improved employee morale.

Integrated change control The process of coordinating changes across a project.

Internal audit A review that identifies opportunities for improvement and proposes solutions.

Internal rate of return (IRR) The annual return that a project delivers, which takes into account the time value of money.

Interpersonal skill The ability to work effectively with others.

Issue A risk that has been realized during the project.

Issue list A list of the project concerns that have been encountered, whether open, in progress, or closed.

Issue management An action involved identifying, recording, evaluating, and controlling the adverse consequences of a problem.

Kick-off meeting An initial meeting to begin a project, bringing together key project stakeholders.

Lag The delay between the end of a predecessor task and the beginning of a successor task.

Lagging A task relationship in which one task must await the start and partial completion of another.

Latest finish The latest time that an activity can be finished without extending the end date for a project.

Latest start The latest time an activity can begin without delaying the project.

Lead The amount of overlap between the end of one task and the beginning of another.

Lessons learned The knowledge gained from the process of completing a project successfully.

Leveling The process of delaying tasks to eliminate resource overallocations caused by two or more tasks using the same resource at the same time.

Life cycle The life of a product or service, usually divided into sequential phases that include initiation, development, execution, operation, maintenance, and termination.

Link A dependency between tasks: finish-to-start, start-to-start, finish-to-finish, or start-to-finish.

Loop A point in a process when the path may need to be repeated based on verification, decision, or repetition.

Management by walking around (MBWA) A management style that uses an unstructured approach to hands-on, direct interaction by managers with their team members. Also called management by wandering around.

Maslow's hierarchy of needs A hierarchy that identifies what people need in their lives, with five levels: physiological, safety, social, esteem, and self-actualization.

Master schedule A timetable that identifies the major activities and milestones.

Material resource The materials consumed during a project.

Matrix organization An organization in which project managers and functional managers share responsibility for assigning resources to tasks and supervising people's work.

Maximum exposure See cash hole.

McGregor's theory of X and Y A management theory that classifies workers into two groups. Type X individuals are dislike work and responsibly and need authoritative management. Type Y people enjoy work and taking on new tasks.

Mediation A method of resolving disputes in which two parties who disagree meet with an impartial judge who tries to help the parties find a compromise.

Methodology A set of standards, techniques, and guidelines used for performing any process.

Milestone A critical date, usually when an especially important deliverable must be delivered.

Milestone reviews The decision points in the life cycle at which the project is presented to stakeholders and approved to move forward to the next step in the process.

Monitoring The process of comparing actual progress against planned progress.

Net present value The value of the project expressed in today's dollars based on the percentage rate the organization uses for the time value of money.

Network analysis The process that identifies the start and finish dates for uncompleted portions of project activities.

Network diagram A left-to-right flowchart showing tasks, areas of responsibility, and time requirements for a project.

Norming In Bruce Tuckman's model of team development, norming is the third phase of development, marked by the establishment of group agreement and clarity of purpose.

Organizational planning The process of identifying, documenting, and assigning project roles, responsibilities, and reporting relationships.

Organizational skill The ability to communicate with other units, knowledge of the political landscape of the company, and possession of a network.

Outline A hierarchical representation of the tasks for a project.

Outsourcing A business practice of moving work to another company, typically in search of cost reductions.

Overtime The amount of work assigned beyond a person's regular working time.

Payback period The time a project takes to earn back what the organization pays to complete the project.

Percent complete The percentage of task duration completed, calculated by dividing the actual duration by the scheduled duration.

Percent work complete The percentage of work completed, calculated by dividing the actual work by the estimated work.

Performance criteria A variety of standards used to evaluate variance from the scope, schedule, and cost baselines.

Performance evaluation and review technique (PERT) A system employed for project scheduling, in which time requirements are weighted to demonstrate the overall time demands of the project.

Performance reporting The process of collecting and disseminating project performance information.

Performing In Bruce Tuckman's model of team development, performing is the fourth phase of development, marked by a strong degree of team unity and autonomy.

Plan A forecast of future events.

Planned value The baseline cost up to the status date for tasks as they were scheduled in the project plan.

Planning The phase that breaks the project into manageable portions and plans how best to proceed.

Planning process The project management process in which users develop plans on how to complete the project.

Portfolio A series of projects with the goal of creating maximum value for the organization.

Predecessor A task that controls the start or finish of another task.

Process The gradual changes that lead toward a result.

Process owner The individual or department that benefits from an improved process or system, or that is involved directly with the input, processing, or output.

Procurement The process of acquiring products, services, and results from outside the project team to complete the project.

Product The result of a project undertaken to produce it.

Productivity A measure of the efficiency of a resource to deliver a specified product within a defined budget and timescale.

Program A group of related projects managed in a coordinated way.

Project A unique, one-time work effort with a defined start and end, the objectives of which are set in advance and are to be achieved by the use of finite resources.

Project board The group of senior stakeholders that will make decisions.

Project charter A document that states the need for the project and defines its results.

Project closure The final stage of a project.

Project control manual A binder where project documents are stored.

Project evaluation and review technique (PERT) A technique that helps identify the critical path, duration, and floats of dependent project activities.

Project initiation A stage during which the necessary preparations are made to justify and plan the project, and to put in place the management environment that will serve as its foundation.

Project initiation document A document summarizing the what, when, how, who, and why of the project.

Project life cycle The series of stages that allows the project team to control the progress of a project.

Project management The processes involved in managing a project, requiring the application of planning, teambuilding, communicating, controlling, decision-making, and closing skills, using specific tools and techniques.

Project manager The person responsible for managing a project's planning and performance.

Project organization chart A diagram showing people involved in a project, including the project team, stakeholders, and resources.

Project overview A short document that identifies why a project will be performed, the business value it provides, and what work it entails.

Project plan A document that describes a project and the plan for completing it and achieving its objectives.

Project plan development The process of integrating and coordinating all project plans to create a single, consistent, coherent document.

Project plan execution The process of performing the activities included in the project plan.

Project sign-off The official confirmation that a project has been completed successfully.

Project team The team responsible for delivering the project itself; the team may consist of people from different organizations.

Project/business value The benefits that completing the project will bring to the organization.

Proposal A written document prepared by vendors that make an offer for consideration.

Purchase order A short form authorizing the purchase of goods from a vendor.

Quality The degree of excellence inherent in the project's product and process.

Quality assurance A process for evaluating project performance in relation to the specified standard of quality.

Quality control A procedure designed to improve quality and reduce defects in a process.

RACI chart A chart that defines each role, with the legend of responsible, accountable, consult, and inform for each activity. Also called a responsibilities matrix.

Repetition loop A process in which completed tasks are moved to the next step and incomplete tasks are returned for further processing.

Request for information (RFI) A request made during the project planning phase to identify specifications from vendors.

Request for proposal (RFP) A solicitation, often made through a bidding process, by a company interested in procurement of a commodity, service, or asset to potential vendors to submit business proposals.

Request for quotation (RFQ) A process whose purpose is to invite vendors to bid on specific products or services.

Reserve A provision in the plan to mitigate cost or schedule risk.

Resource The people, technology, space, and tools needed to complete project tasks and deliverables.

Resource leveling The process of reassigning work so that overloaded staff have a more manageable workload.

Resource planning The process of determining what people, equipment, and materials, are needed to perform project activities.

Resource pool A set of resources available to work on project tasks.

Resource requirements The list of the type and quantity of each person, role, skill, material, and equipment needed to complete the project.

Responsibilities matrix A chart that lists members of the project team and shows their responsibilities. Also called an RACI chart.

Risk The possibility of the occurrence of an event that will negatively affect the project.

Risk assessment The process of constructing a list of specific potential problems and threats discovered while identifying and quantifying risks.

Risk evaluation The process of determining whether a risk is worthy of the investment needed to mitigate it.

Risk management The control, planning, and preventive measures required to prevent threats.

Risk response The steps, procedures, or techniques to implement if a risk occurs.

Risk response plan A document detailing identified risks, their probability of occurrence, possible impacts on objectives, and the proposed response to each risk.

Rolling wave A planning approach in which only the near future is planned in detail; work further out is only planned at a high level.

Schedule The document prepared by the team to map steps in the project and track progress toward a specified completion date.

Schedule control The means of controlling changes to the project schedule.

Schedule development The process of analyzing activity sequences, activity durations, and resource requirements to create the project schedule.

Schedule variance (SV) The budgeted cost of work performed (earned value) minus the budgeted cost of work scheduled (planned value).

Scope The description of the work that is and is not included in the project.

Scope change control A method of controlling changes to the project scope.

Scope creep The ways in which projects grow beyond their original scope.

Scope definition The process of subdividing the deliverables into smaller components to provide better control.

Scope management plan A plan that provides an analysis of the stability and reliability of the scope of the project

Scope planning The process of elaborating the work of the project and developing the scope statement.

Scope statement A document used to confirm an understanding of project scope among the stakeholders, used as a basis for making future decisions. Also called a statement of work.

Scope verification The process of formalizing acceptance of the project scope.

Self-assessment A process in which a person identifies his or her goals, strengths, and failings as a member of the project team.

Skills assessment The process in which a project manager notes and measures the skills of each of his or her team members.

Skills matrix A list of the skills of each team member that quantifies those skills as beginning, advanced, or expert.

Slack The amount of time a task can slip without impacting the finish date of the project.

Sponsor The senior supporter of the project, responsible for ensuring that there are sufficient resources and championing the business value the project will deliver to the organization.

Staff acquisition The process of getting needed human resources assigned to and working on a project.

Staffing management plan A plan used to determine staff levels and scheduling.

Stage A period within in a project that has an identified start date, end date, budget, and deliverables.

Stakeholder Any department, organization, or individual with a direct interest in the project and its outcome.

Standard rate The rate charged by a person for regular work hours.

Start date The date that a task is scheduled to start, based on its predecessors.

Start-to-finish A task relationship in which the second task cannot finish until the start of the first task.

Start-to-start A task relationship in which one task must start at the same time as another.

Statement of work A project document that lists, in some measure of detail, what the project entails and what it will deliver. Also called a scope statement.

Status report A summary report that is provided by the project team for the stakeholders to keep them informed about project-related issues, deliverables, and timelines.

Status review meeting A regularly scheduled meeting of project stakeholders to exchange information about the project.

Steering committee A small group of senior executives who approve, prioritize, and monitor projects.

Storming In Bruce Tuckman's model of team development, storming is the second phase of project team growth, featuring low team unity and challenges to a project manager's authority.

Subject-matter expert An expert in a special field of study.

Success criteria The list of conditions that must be met for a project to be deemed successful.

Successor A task with a start or finish date that depends on another task.

Summary task A task that summarizes the dates, duration, and work of all its subordinate tasks.

SWOT analysis An examination of strengths, weaknesses, opportunities, and threats that can be conducted at the start of a project as part of the risk management process.

Tangible benefit A quantifiable benefit that may be directly related to the financial objectives.

Task An activity undertaken to achieve deliverables.

Team development The process that develops individual and group competencies to enhance project performance.

Team room A physical space dedicated to project teamwork.

Time schedule A representation of a project's timescale.

Top-down estimating A method used at the commencement of a project to obtain a high-level forecast of its timescale, cost, and deliverables.

Total slack The amount of time a task and its successors can slip without delaying the project finish date.

Transition phase A phase in change management theory where all the work gets done—that is, the actions that take the project from its current state to the future state.

Triple constraint A framework to evaluate competing demands of time, cost, and scope, usually depicted as a triangle.

Underspend A term used to describe when not all of the planned budget has been spent or is forecast to be spent.

Unfavorable variance The condition when actual expenses are higher than the budget for a specified period or activity.

Validation The process of checking that a project has met the underlying business need that it was intended to fulfill.

Value creation The expression of the business benefit of a project, in terms of either cost savings, efficiency gains, increased sales, or reduced risk.

Value chain A concept defining levels of both quality control and process management, used to ensure both value and quality as part of the improved result.

Variance The amount by which the total cost of a line item differs from its projected cost.

Verification The process of checking that a project has delivered the scope that was promised; it differs from validation in that it focuses on what was promised and what was delivered, rather than the underlying business problem to be solved.

Verification loop A pattern within a process in which an outcome is checked; if the result is correct, the process continues, and if it is not, the outcome is returned to be revised.

Virtual team A team with members who are not located in the same office and rely on technology to communicate and finish a project.

Weak link A location within a process where errors are likely to occur, usually found when processes are passed from one area of responsibility to another.

Weekly status report A one-page report written by the project manager that provides a snapshot of the project's status.

Work The time units required to complete a task.

Work authorization system A formal procedure to ensure project work is sanctioned, and done at the right time and in the right sequence.

Work breakdown structure (WBS) A charting system used to identify the tasks of a project with flowcharts.

Work package A task representing the actual work that resources do; it appears at the lowest level of the WBS.

Work resource A resource, such as a person or equipment, that is scheduled for the time worked on a project.

Work results The outcome of an activity associated with a project.

Workaround The development of alternatives in response to a problem.

APPENDIX E

Templates

SWOT Analysis Template

	Helpful	Harmful
Internal	**Strengths**	**Weaknesses**
External	**Opportunities**	**Threats**

Project Scope Statement Template

Project Name:	Projected start:
Completed by:	Projected duration:

Project Purpose:

Project Description:

Desired Results:

Exclusions:

Communication Needs:

Acceptance Criteria:

Constraints:

Approvals:

Stakeholder Interview Template

Interviewee:	Date:
Interviewer:	

Project Purpose

Description of Deliverables

Desired Results

Exclusions (items out of scope)

Communication Needs (who, how, and how often)

Acceptance Criteria (who needs to sign off on what, and how they will sign off)

Constraints

Project Roster Template

Name	Title	Department	Specialty	Role	Phone	Email	Notes

Responsibility Matrix Template

	Role	Role	Role	Role	Role	Role	Role
Task							
Task							
Task							
Task							
Task							
Task							
Task							

Project Milestones Template

Milestone	Responsibility	Date

WBS Task Template

Task	Subtasks	Subtasks Level 2	Subtasks Level 3
Total Duration			

Change Request Form Template

Change Request Assigned Change Request Number: _____	
☐ Approved	☐ Rejected
Project Name:	
Date Change Requested:	
Description of Requested Change:	
Justification for Change:	
Cost Impact:	
Schedule Impacts:	
Other Impacts:	
Comments:	
Submitted By:	
Project Sponsor Signature and Date:	
Project Manager Signature and Date:	

Change Log Template

Project Name					
Project Manager					
Change ID	Date Submitted	Requested by	Description	Impact	Status

Communication Plan Template

Project Name				
Project Manager				
Stakeholder	Information Needs	Frequency	Medium	Response

Meeting Agenda Template

Meeting Agenda		
Project		
Purpose		
Date		
Time		
Place		
Invitees		
Time	Agenda Item	Lead
Notes		

Weekly Status Report Template

Name:	Project:
Tasks started this week:	
Tasks scheduled to start this did not: Why did these tasks not start on schedule?	
Tasks completed this week:	
Tasks scheduled to complete that did not: Why did these tasks not finish on schedule?	
Plans for next week:	
Note any current or pending problems:	

Final Project Report Template

Final Project Report	
Project Name:	Completion Date:
Executive Summary	
Project Background	
Major Project Activities	
Project Results	
Key Project Changes	
Project Challenges	
Transition to Operations	
Matters Outstanding	

Lessons Learned Template

Lessons Learned		
Project Name:	Project Manager:	Date Prepared:
Project Start Date:	Original Project End Date:	Actual Project End Date:
Prepared By:	Prepared Date:	
What contributed to the success of the project?		
What hindered success?		
Project Characteristics		
Was the project planned properly?		
Were users involved in planning?		
Were risks identified and managed?		
Were contingency plans developed?		
Was the decision structure clear?		
Was communication timely?		
Lessons Learned		
What could have been done differently?		
Why was it not done?		
Where will these Lessons Learned be stored for retrieval by others?		

REFERENCES

Afshari, F., Jones, R., 2007. Developing an integrated institutional repository at Imperial College London. Program: Electronic Library and Information Systems 41 (4), 338–352.

Albrecht, K.H., 2007. Campus-Wide Digital Image Databases: The Impossible Dream? VRA Bulletin 34 (3), 51–54.

Bak, G., Armstrong, P., 2009. Points of convergence: seamless long-term access to digital publications and archival records at library and archives Canada. Archival Science 8 (4), 279–293.

Black, G., 2005. The Engaging Museum: Developing Museums for Visitor Involvement. Routledge, New York.

Bloss, A., Lanier, D., November 1997. The Library Department Head in the context of matrix management and reengineering. College & Research Libraries 499–507.

Bolton, B., 2005. 10 tips for becoming a successful manager. InformationWeek 1025 (64).

Brasley, S.S., 2008. Effective librarian and discipline faculty collaboration models for integrating information literacy into the fabric of an academic institution. New Directions for Teaching and Learning 114, 71–88.

Brooks Jr., F.P., 1995. The Mythical Man-Month: Essays on Software Engineering Anniversary Edition. Addison-Wesley, New York.

Carpenter, J., 2010. Project Management in Libraries, Archives and Museums: Working with Government and Other External Partners. Chandos, Oxford.

Cervone, H.F., 2004. How not to run a digital library project. OCLC Systems & Services 20 (4), 162–166.

Cervone, H.F., 2005. Influencing: a critical skill for managing digital library project teams. OCLC Systems & Services 21 (2), 105–109.

Cervone, H.F., 2009. Strategic analysis for digital library development. OCLC Systems & Services: International Digital Library Perspectives 25 (1), 16–19.

Chambers, S., Perrow, D., 1998. Introducing project management techniques to the Robinson Library, University of Newcastle. Journal of Librarianship & Information Science 30 (4), 249–258.

Chang, M., 2010. An agile approach to library IT innovations. Library Hi Tech 28 (4), 672–689.

Choi, Y., Rasmussen, E., 2009. What qualifications and skills are important for digital librarian positions in academic libraries? A job advertisement analysis. Journal of Academic Librarianship 35 (5), 457–467.

Closing the Gap: The Link Between Project Management Excellence and Long-Term Success, 2009. Economist Intelligence Unit, London.

Davis, D., 2005. New projects: beware of false economies. In: Harvard Business Review on Managing Projects. Harvard Business School Publishing, Boston, pp. 19–39.

Doan, T., Kennedy, M.L., 2009. Innovation, creativity, and meaning: leading in the Information Age. Journal of Business and Finance Librarianship 14 (4), 348–358.

Dojka, J., 1990. The Yale University archives. Case Studies in Archives Program Development. American Archivist 53, 548–560.

Duncan, V., Gerrard, A., 2011. All together now! integrated virtual reference in the academic library. Reference & User Services Quarterly 50 (3), 280–292.

Elbeik, S., Thomas, M., 1998. Project Skills. Butterworth-Heinemann, Oxford.

Fagan, J.C., Keach, J.A., 2011. Managing web projects in academic libraries. Library & Leadership Management 25 (3), 1–22.

Fagerlund, L., 1990. The Utah State archives. Case Studies in Archives Program Development. American Archivist 53, 548–560.

Feeney, M., Sult, L., 2011. Project management in practice: implementing a process to ensure accountability and success. Journal of Library Administration 51, 744–763.

Fowler, M., Highsmith, J., 2001. The agile manifesto. Software Development 9 (8), 28–32.

Frame, J.D., 1987. Managing Projects in Organizations: How to Make the Best Use of Time, Techniques, and People. Jossey-Bass, San Francisco.

Griffin, R., 2012. Fundamentals of Management, sixth ed. South-Western Cengage Learning, Mason, OH.

Gulliver, F.R., March 1987. Post-project appraisals pay. Harvard Business Review 128–130.

Hackman, L.J., 1990. Introduction and commentary. Case Studies in Archives Program Development. American Archivist 53, 548–560.

Herzberg, F., January–February 1968. One more time: how do you motivate employees? Harvard Business Review 53–62.

Horwath, J.A., 2012. How do we manage? project management in libraries: an investigation. Partnership: The Canadian Journal of Library and Information Practice and Research 7 (1), 1–34.

Hosker, R., Knowles, C., Rodger, N., 2015. Integrated skills, integrated data: mapping best practice and collections for innovation and engagement. International Conference on Integrated Information. AIP Conference Proceedings 1644 (1), 153–160.

Iyer, H., 2009. A profession in transition: towards development and implementation of standards for visual resources management. Part A – the organization's perspective. Information Research 14 (3).

Johnson, H., 1994. Strategic planning for modern libraries. Library Management 15 (1), 7–18.

Katzenbach, J.R., Smith, D.K., March–April 1993. The discipline of teams. Harvard Business Review 111–120.

Kinkus, J., 2007. Project management skills: a literature review and content analysis of librarian position announcements. College & Research Libraries 68 (4), 352–363.

Kirchhoff, T., Schweibenz, W., Sieglerschmidt, J., 2008. Archives, libraries, museums, and the spell of ubiquitous knowledge. Archival Science 8 (4), 251–266.

Lai, L.-L., 2005. Educating knowledge professionals in library and information science schools. Journal of Educating Media & Library Sciences 42 (3), 347–362.

Larson, C.E., Lafasto, F.M.J., 1989. Teamwork: What Must Go Right, What Can Go Wrong. Sage, Newberry Park, CA.

Leifer, R., McDermott, C.M., O'Connor, G.C., Peters, L.S., Rice, M., Veryzer, R.W., 2000. Radical Innovation: How Mature Companies Can Outsmart Upstarts. Harvard Business School Press, Boston.

Lipnack, J., Stamps, J., 2000. Virtual Teams: Reaching Across Space, Time, and Organizations with Technology. Wiley, New York.

Mackenzie, M.L., Smith, J.P., 2009. Management education for library directors: are graduate library programs providing future library directors with the skills and knowledge they will need? Journal of Education for Library and Information Science 50 (3), 129–142.

Maslow, A., 1943. A theory of human motivation. Psychological Review 50 (4), 370–396.

Massis, B.E., 2010. Project management in the library. New Library World 111 (11/12), 526–529.

Mathews, J.M., Pardue, H., 2009. The presence of IT skill sets in librarian position announcements. College & Research Libraries 70 (3), 250–257.

McGregor, D., 1960. The Human Side of Enterprise. McGraw-Hill, New York.

Munduate, L., Media, F., 2009. Organizational change. In: Tjosvold, D., Wisse, B. (Eds.), Power and Interdependence in Organizations. Cambridge University Press, Cambridge, pp. 299–316.

O'Toole, J.M., 1990. The archdiocese of Boston. Case Studies in Archives Program Development. American Archivist 53, 548–560.

Parker, G.M., 2003. Cross-Functional Teams: Working with Allies, Enemies, and Other Strangers. Jossey-Bass, San Francisco.

PMI's Pulse of the Profession: The High Cost of Low Performance 2013, 2013. Project Management Institute, Newtown Square, PA.

Project Management Institute, 2006. Practice Standard for Work Breakdown Structures. Project Management Institute, Newtown Square, PA.

Royer, I., 2005. Why bad projects are so hard to kill. In: Harvard Business Review on Managing Projects. Harvard Business School Publishing, Boston, pp. 85–108.

Schachter, D., 2004. Managing your library's technology projects. Information Outlook 8 (12), 10–12.

Schaefer, Lu E., 2000. How to Make Remote Teams Works. Training materials from a seminar given to Hewlett-Packard in Palo Alto.

Schreiber, B., Shannon, J., 2001. Developing library leaders for the 21st century. Journal of Library Administration 32, 35–57.

Stanton, J.M., Kim, Y., Oakleft, M., David Lankes, R., Gandel, P., Cogburn, D., Liddy, E.D., 2011. Education for e-science professionals: job analysis, curriculum guidance, and program considerations. Journal of Education for Library and Information Science 52 (2), 79–94.

Staw, B.M., Ross, J., 2005. Knowing when to pull the plug. In: Harvard Business Review on Managing Projects. Harvard Business School Publishing, Boston, pp. 65–84.

Stoffle, C.J., Cuillier, C., 2011. From surviving to thriving. Journal of Library Administration 51, 130–155.

Tuckman, B., 1965. Development sequence in small groups. Psychological Bulletin 63, 384–389.

Vinopal, J., 2012. Project portfolio management for academic libraries: a gentle introduction. College & Research Libraries 73 (4), 379–389.

Wamsley, L.H., 2009. Controlling project chaos: project management for library staff. PNLA Quarterly 73 (2), 5–6, 27.

Weingand, D.E., 1997. Customer Service Excellence: A Concise Guide for Librarians. American Library Association, Chicago.

Whiteman, B., 2007. Cooperative collection building: a response to Gerald Beasley. RBM: A Journal of Rare Books, Manuscripts, and Cultural Heritage 8 (1), 29–34.

Winston, M.D., Hoffman, T., 2005. Project management in libraries. Journal of Library Administration 42 (1), 51–61.

Woolridge, B., Schmid, T., Floyd, S.W., 2008. The middle management perspective on strategy process. Journal of Management 34 (6), 1190–1221.

Wysocki, R.K., 2011. The Business Analyst/Project Manager: A New Partnership for Managing Complexity and Uncertainty. John Wiley & Sons, Hoboken, NJ.

INDEX

Note: Page numbers followed by "f" and "t" indicate figures and tables, respectively.

Printed in the United States
By Bookmasters